THE PARSON'S TALE

Geoffrey Chaucer
1340 – 1400

Geoffrey Chaucer's

THE PARSON'S TALE

from THE CANTERBURY TALES

Translated from the Middle English

with Original Illustrations,
Introduction, Notes, Chronology
and Bibliography

by

Mary Farrell Pomerleau

Carnegie Mellon, M. A.

CHARLEMAGNE PRESS
Arcadia
MCMXCV

The Charlemagne Press with the services of Littlejon Publications of Santa Monica, California produced this book. Axel Müllers of Aachen, Germany travelled to Canterbury Cathedral to take the photographs used on the cover. The English Gothic design of the ceiling of the Cathedral is used on the Front Cover of the book.

ISBN - 0-944455-05-0

ACKNOWLEDGEMENTS

To the English Department of Emmanuel College and to the Graduate School of Carnegie-Mellon University, and especially to Dr. John Hart, who, as my Tutor, supervised my Master's Thesis on *Dryden's Translation of Chaucer*, much gratitude is owed.

The primary source for this translation was the textbook in which I began my study of Chaucer half a century ago, *The Complete Works of Chaucer*, edited by Professor F. N. Robinson of Harvard University, printed at the Riverside Press in Cambridge in 1933. Later editions, while helpful for textual criticism, were not needed for this translation. Other scholarly texts such as those of W. W. Skeats (Oxford) and J. M. Manly (Chicago) had been consulted by Professor Robinson for his First Edition.

For commentary and criticism of the complete *Canterbury Tales* (which, however, is not the scope of this present volume) no book can equal Helen Cooper's recent volume in the *Oxford Guides to Chaucer,* 1989, Oxford University Press, England.

A debt of gratitude is owed to the author and journalist, Charles A. Coulombe, who encouraged me to make my translation available to a wider scholastic and collegiate audience.

CONTENTS

PREFACE   9

INTRODUCTION   13

THE PARSON'S TALE   31

APPENDICES   143
   Notes   145
   Chronology   149
   Glossary   151
   Bibliography   155

ILLUSTRATIONS
   Geoffrey Chaucer   2
   The Parson   30
   Pride   58
   Humility   66
   Envy   70
   Charity   72
   Anger   76
   Patience   88
   Sloth   92
   Fortitude   97
   Avarice   100
   Generosity   107
   Gluttony   109
   Moderation   111
   Lechery   114
   Chastity   122
   Canterbury Cathedral   134

PREFACE

The modern English Language owes much of its present form to three documents: the King James *Bible*, the *Book of Common Prayer*, and the works of William Shakespeare. Of these, the first two are translations (albeit with a Protestant orientation) of the scriptures and liturgy which dominated Medieval Europe. In that sense, they do not reflect the work of one man, or one era. Shakespeare's plays and poetry, on the other hand, do reflect the work of a single genius; a genius whose understanding not only of his own times (or the audiences of those times), but of the immutable human condition in general, has never been excelled since. Indeed, in his insight into human nature and psychology, he had perhaps only one rival. In this rival we see the same ability to delineate types of character, to bring his creations alive on the page precisely because they are the sort of people who actually walk and breathe on this planet. Moreover, this rival accomplished in one major work what Shakespeare did in the whole of his endeavor. The rival is **Geoffrey Chaucer**, and the work is *The Canterbury Tales*.

Chaucer depicted for us in his *Tales* late Medieval England with a clarity the best histories do not possess. On the one hand, the ethos of that age, so different from our own due to the prevailing philosophy (well described by Mrs. Pomerleau in her Introduction) comes alive. Within that context, however, we may recognize portrayed all the unchanging human types who populate our modern world --- even ourselves.

When the *Tales* are well taught, there are few High School or College students who will not fall in love with one or more of Chaucer's pilgrims. Indeed, the Wife of Bath and the Knight were my own favorites in school. But whatever edition of the *Tales* is used, and whichever character's stories are read, one is almost always left out --- the Parson. His tale is summarized, usually, with a curt dismissal. After all, we are generally told, his

9

"tale" is really just a sermon reflecting an outdated theological or moral system. There are four problems with this view.

The first is that, as Mrs. Pomerleau tells us, without *The Parson's Tale* our view of Chaucer is unbalanced and inaccurate. The Parson's piety is as much a part of the pilgrim's world as the Wife of Bath's bawdiness or the Pardoner's hypocrisy. To eliminate this aspect is to vitiate study of the entire work.

Secondly, the objection to the Parson's belief system as irrelevant because outmoded is incorrect. What is *Hamlet,* but an exposition of the doctrine of Purgatory ? What could we do with the whole of Medieval literature ? *Beowulf, Chanson de Roland, Parzival, Le Morte d'Arthur,* to say nothing of Dante --- indeed, the whole of Medieval Romance is animated by precisely the code which the Parson explains comprehensively yet concisely. It is not too much to say that a study of the Parson is essential to a good understanding of these other works.

Moreover, the moral problems he deals with, such topics as social justice, abortion, substance abuse, as well as basic things like personal honesty, are still very much with us. The Parson expresses what was almost completely the majority view of his time on these and other topics. While many today might disagree with the answers he and his peers gave to these problems, surely the modern dialogue concerning such issues can only be enriched by a knowledge of these earlier opinions. In any case, based as they are upon both Classical, Scriptural, and early Christian sources, these views have at least continuity in their favor.

Lastly, just as the Wife of Bath's exuberance and the Pardoner's hypocrisy are not unknown today (together with the virtues and vices exemplified by the other pilgrims) so too, there are such folk as the Parson about even in our time. Certainly, in Chaucer's description of the Parson, we might see someone like Mother Teresa, just as others might see Mahatma Gandhi or the Dalai Lama. That is to say, the Parson is exhibited as a genuinely good person, as someone who truly lives for others --- a type we moderns respect just as much as our ancestors did. In the course of his tale, the Parson enunciates the values which have made him what he is. It is rare indeed that we receive such insight into this kind of person, a kind people of all opinions will admit the world needs more of.

We live in an ever more complex and difficult-to-under-stand society, as Alvin Toffler in *Future Shock* and numerous other authors assure us. Philosophy, ethics, literature, politics --- all seem to be in a neverending state of flux. For the Medievals, however, things were very different. Norman F. Cantor gives a good summary:

> In assessing their own world, medieval intellectuals were heavily conditioned by a persistent idealism that saw in society around them signs of the earthly incarnation of the Heavenly City . . .
>
> The sacred dogma of the Incarnation likewise governed the social perceptions of medieval people. They were pre-conditioned by the dogma of the Incarnation and the philosophy of "realism" that underlies it to find the ideal within the material, the beautiful within the ugly, the moral and peaceful in the midst of violence and disorder. **"The Word was made flesh,** and dwelt among us . . . full of grace and truth." Since everything was of divine creation, medieval intellectuals had no doubt that all the pieces would ultimately fit together in an idealistic, morally committed structure. Whatever they saw or experienced was part of a divine manifestation. (*Inventing the Middle Ages*, page 414.)

Chaucer's Parson epitomizes this world-view. Taken together with the personalities and opinions of the rest of the pilgrims, his *Tale* transforms *The Canterbury Tales* from just a literary masterpiece to a statement of values and ethos for at least thirty generations of Europeans. While we may not share these values, this statement can at least shed light on the world views currently competing for our acceptance.

In making this key work generally available to the modern English speaking public, and by her illuminating Introduction and Notes, Mrs. Pomerleau has done a great service to lovers and students of Chaucer and Medieval Literature.

Charles A. Coulombe
Los Angeles, California
May 8, 1995

INTRODUCTION

INTRODUCTION

THE PARSON AND HIS TALE

A good man was there of religion,
He was a poor parson of a town,
But rich he was in holy thought and work;
He was also a learned man, a clerk,*
That the Christian Gospel would truly preach,
And his parishioners devoutly would he teach.

Benign, he was and very diligent,
And in adversity, full patient,
As often he was proved in this wise.
He was full loath to demand his tithes*
But rather he would give, without a doubt,
To his poor parishioners, all about
From his own alms* and his own subsistence.

He could in little things have forbearance.
Wide was his parish with houses wide asunder
But he did not neglect, in rain or thunder,
In sickness nor in troubles to visit
The farthest in his parish, great and slight,
Upon foot, and in his hand a stave.*
This noble example to his sheep he gave,
That first he acted and afterward he taught
Out of the Gospel, he the meaning caught,
And this figure he added also thereto,
That if gold rust, what shall iron do ?
For if a priest be foul, in whom we trust.
No wonder if a common man will rust;
And shame it is if a priest be seen
As a foul shepherd and the sheep clean.

Well ought a priest a good example give,
By his cleanness, how his sheep should live.

He never left his parish to hire*
And left his sheep struggling in the mire
While he ran to London to Saint Paul's
To get money for praying for souls
Or with a guild* to be retained.
But stayed at home and kept his fold contained
So that the wolf could not them harry.
He was a shepherd and not a mercenary.

And though he was holy and virtuous
He was not to sinful men contemptuous
Nor in his speech mean nor scornful,
But in his teaching, discreet and thoughtful
To draw people to heaven by fairness,
And by good example; this was his business.
But if any person were obstinate
Whether he were of high or low estate,*
Him would he rebuke sharply, right there.
A better priest I trust there is nowhere.
He wanted no pomp and reverence,
Nor did he have a scrupulous conscience.
But Christ's doctrine and his apostles twelve
He taught, but first he followed it himself.

(Lines 476-526, General Prologue.)   See Note 1.
Words marked with an asterisk are explained in the Glossary.

Thus does Chaucer describe his Parson in the General Prologue to *The Canterbury Tales*. His total approval of this good priest who practices what he preaches is evident. More subtle is the condemnation of all priests who do not as the Parson does, who preach one thing and do another themselves, who are anxious for recognition and pomp, who are respecters of persons of high estate, who are disdainful of sinners, who are greedy for money, who seek important parishes or benefices, who neglect the poor, who are lazy, who are lustful, etc.

The Parson, the Knight, and the Ploughman are the only pilgrims of the thirty in the *Tales* who escape Chaucer's acerbic wit. Each of these three represents one of the medieval "estates." The Parson is the best of the clergy, the Knight is the best of the nobility, the Ploughman, brother to the Parson, is the best of the workers. The Knight is the first story teller and the Parson, in all significant editions, whatever the other arrangements, is always the last, by design, as the words of the Host in the Parson's prologue show: "For every man, save thou, hath told his tale" (Parson's Prologue Line 25) .

Chaucer did not finish all the tales he indicated to us in the General Prologue. The reason is open to speculation but it is clear that he had some structure in mind (2). *The Parson's Tale* is integral to this stucture. It underscores all the other tales by sharpening the concept of pilgrimage, not only to the tomb of St. Thomas à Becket at Canterbury (3) but the pilgrimage of life to the "heavenly Jerusalem," as the Parson points out in his Prologue (line 51) and throughout his tale. For this reason, it is sad that so many modern tranlations omit *The Parson's Tale,* passing it off as a long, boring treatise on the seven deadly sins, written in prose and too heavy to be of interest. To a person who loves Chaucer and finds the medieval mind remarkable, *The Parson's Tale* is neither boring nor uninteresting.

Recently a friend asked me to translate *The Parson's Tale* for his research. He found that in six current editions of *The Canterbury Tales* in modern English not one included this tale. Even the Everyman and Book of the Month Club editions of *The Canterbury Tales* in Middle English excluded this tale (4).

Although twenty-five years have passed since I did my work on Chaucer in Carnegie Mellon's rare book room, I found the same absolute delight in reading the sharp, clear words as I felt as a graduate student. I thought how sad that so many people think of "The Father of English Literature" only as a poet, a witty teller of sometimes bawdy stories, like *The Miller's Tale*, and a satirist of human nature. Chaucer was all that but he was much more. Some know he wrote romances. Some know he was member of Parliament and in the service of three kings. Few appreciate his depth and intelligence as a translator of Boethius' *Consolations of Philosophy* (5), and a scholar capable of transposing the technical treatises of Saint Raymond of Penneforte and William Peraldous (6) into the voice of a simple country priest.

To find *The Parson's Tale* left out of *The Canterbury Tales* is like putting together a beautiful picture puzzle, only to discover that three central pieces of the picture have been left out. Missing is the piece that shows the underlying viewpoint that ties all the odd assortment of medieval travelers to a fellowship closer than we can imagine. It is the piece that shows how the pilgrims could accept as a fellow pilgrim a hypocrite like the contemptible Pardoner or the Monk or Friar, or any of them, for that matter, and how these people saw their own transgressions. Also missing is the piece that shows the author's search for structure. Finally, missing is the piece revealing the inner heart of Chaucer himself, who ended the whole work with the *Retractions*, a few lines so curious to some critics that they consider it another of his jokes or perhaps some scribe's interpolation. These would provide the frame of reference needed to appreciate the whole work.

FIRST MISSING PIECE
THE MEDIEVAL VIEWPOINT

The medieval mind was a long way from the mind that is reflected in *USA Today*. It saw Truth as an absolute, not relative to what one believed it to be. If it filled one with consolation or if it filled one with consternation. Truth did not change. Men change, circumstances change, weather changes. To the Medieval mind, there was such a thing as sin. It began with the Original Sin of Adam and Eve. All mankind, their descendants, must be baptized "with water and the Holy Spirit"(7), as Jesus said in the Gospel and Saint Paul reiterated, to attain salvation. But there remains a taint on all mankind; no one is perfect. All men are tempted by sin. The Parson says, "And this thing may not fail as long as he live; it may well grow feeble and weaken by virtue of baptism and by the grace of God through penitence" (line 340 ff.). In sinning we offend not only each other (as the emphasis is given today) or ourselves (as others affirm), but primarily as the Parson emphasized over and over with each sin described, the all good and loving God who is ever ready to forgive those who are sorry, no matter how horrible their sins. However, as the Parson also points out, in sinning without repentance, we choose for ourselves an eternity with the devils in an Inferno not unlike that described by Dante. This is the absolute on which the Parson focuses. It was clear to all the pilgrims that, not only were the Pardoner and the Miller less than perfect, they themselves all were. They needed all the grace they could get; hence the pilgrimage.

The philosophy which pervaded the medieval mind, in England especially, in that period was still that of St. Augustine rather than the more recent philosophy of St. Thomas Aquinas. St. Augustine was influenced by Plato rather than Aristotle (8). He was what Neo-Thomistic scholars call an **"ultra-realist;"** that is to say he believed in the reality of Universals*. Truth is Truth even if no man believes it. To the medieval mind, the concepts of good works and sin, just reward, and just punishment, heaven and hell were realities. Order in the Universe was a reality coming from and sustained by the mind of God. Life was real, death was real, life after death was real.

To this mind the Communion of Saints* was a reality. A pilgrimage to the tomb of Saint Thomas was neither a superstition nor a vacation trip. It was like a trip to ask one's older

brother, a favorite of the Father's, to put in a good word about
one's needs. To this mind which saw the Incarnation* of God
as the ultimate reality, the body was a holy thing that would be
resurrected, glorified and united to the soul after death. It was
worthy of great dignity. The body of a saint like Thomas à
Becket was a very holy thing, surely, in the eyes of Almighty
God and, therefore, a source of grace to those on earth.

The Wife of Bath might have had a notion in the back of her
mind that she would find husband number six on the pilgrimage;
the Pardoner might have had an idea he could find plenty of
fervent souls who would be susceptible to what the Parson calls
"foolish largesse.*" But they did not fool themselves into think-
ing that they were not sinners or not in the need of the grace of
this pilgrimage, the intercession of Saint Thomas. Thus the
Host speaks for all of them at the end of the Parson's Prologue:

> "Be fructus, and that in little space
> And to do well God sende you His grace."

Helen Cooper states so well, "Thus he gives the secular
world's blessing on the Parson. Secular and spiritual are not in
opposition: they are all traveling the same road and are eager to
end in 'some virtuous sentence' " (9) (Cooper, p. 397).

SECOND MISSING PIECE
STRUCTURE

As for the second missing piece, it is Chaucer's search for
structure. It seems as if all artists are obsessed with this search:
structure in their work, structure in their lives, structure in the
universe and, especially in our times, structure in their personal
view of the universe. The creative impulse longs for a structure
in its work, even if that work is to reflect chaos. It is found
either in the way the universe is ordered or in the frame man uses
to try to understand it. For Chaucer, structure in the universe
was pretty clear. He lived in a God-centered culture. The diver-
sity of human works, human personalities, human foibles

fascinated him, delighted him, but he saw them as all channeling toward one goal, a life everlasting, "perdurable."*

The *Tales* begin with the beautiful catalog of characters, their particularities spread out before us in a colorful tapestry. Each person is different. Each tale is different and reflective of a unique person. The three estates arc all represented including a gamut of characters from the ploughman to the wealthy merchant class, all rising from the agricultural workers' estate. Their common denominator seems to be found in their desire to make this pilgrimage, their Catholic faith in God, their faith in the sanctity of St. Thomas. All are familiar with the Scriptures and use them to their own intent; the Wife of Bath to justify her way of life, the Pardoner to wring money from the fellow travelers, etc.

The Parson, however, is utterly honest, free from the guiles of fiction and poetry's "rim, ram, rif", and uses the Scriptures to lead the others toward their salvation. His primary appeal is to reason; he teaches rather than persuades. He explains that the reason must be subject to God and then it must take control over the emotions, then emotions over the body, in that hierarchy.

The Parson moves from the concept of the three Estates of that day to a new concept of three Estates, universal to all humankind: "Certainly, the estate of man is in three manners: either it is the estate of innocence as was the estate of Adam before he fell into sin. . . Another estate is that of sinful man . another estate is that of grace; in which estate he remains firm in the works of penitence" (lines 681-684). Thus the structure of the whole *Canterbury Tales* seems to move from the general diversity of human nature at the base of a triangle to the point where human nature is universal, moving upward toward God and the "Jerusalem celestial."

That which points it upward toward the right path is Penitence. **Penitence** is the subject of *The Parson's Tale*. In this way the Tale underscores the work as a whole, giving it an overall structure in keeping with the idea of pilgrimage.

The internal structure of the *Tale* follows a favorite medieval concept: a division into three parts (10). These are

Contrition, Confession, and **Satisfaction**. Contrition is
sorrow for sin; Confession is the formal telling of sin to a
priest; Satisfaction is making amends and doing penance. (11)
The Parson compares Penitence to a tree: Contrition is the root;
Confession is the trunk which has leaves and branches; Satis-
faction is the fruit.

The *Tale* opens with the analogy of a path on a
journey to the celestial Jerusalem, heaven. The way or path
is Penitence. The first 106 lines pertain to Penitence, what
it is, its etymology and its divisions and kinds. The next
section is of those things that pertain to Penitence: Con-
trition, Confession, Satisfaction. Contrition which takes the
reader to line 315 is divided into four main parts: what it
is, what moves a man to be contrite (which is in six parts);
how he should be contrite and what contrition does for the
soul.

Confession is by far the longest part, taking the reader to
line 1027, because here the seven deadly sins, Pride, Envy,
Anger, Sloth, Greed, Gluttony, and Lust, are explained and their
remedies, Humility, Charity, Patience, Fortitude, Generosity,
Moderation, Chastity and Continence, are given. The Parson
divides this whole section into three parts: what confession is,
whether it is necessary, and what is necessary for a true con-
fession. He says that confession is a true showing of one's sins
to the priest along with all the circumstances. He then explains
the seven deadly sins, their sources and varities, and when they
are venial and when mortal, their circumstances, and, finally,
their remedies. With the decorum of the person he is described
to be, he always puts emphasis on the sin and not the sinner,
"not angry at the man, but angry at the misdeed of the man"
(line 540). It is noteworthy that nowhere does the Parson seem
to make any particular rebuke to any of the individual pilgrims.

One might expect that in discussing the selling of reli-
gious treasures, for example, there would be some kind of a side
rebuke to the evil Pardoner, but there is none; he confines
himself to an explanation of simony*. Sometimes it seems to
modern man a negative and depressing attitude to concentrate

mostly on the sins and so little on the "remedies" or opposing virtues. But to confess, it is necessary to know just what is sinful and why and how. In that day, sin was a popular subject for treatises and discussion, especially after the decree of the Lateran IV Council (12).

The lines on satisfaction take the reader to line 1056. Then come the things which hinder penance, taken briefly to line 1075. The tale ends with a brief passage of five lines, about as close as the Parson comes to emotional rhetoric, describing the bliss of heaven as being the fruit of penitence and the goal of life's pilgrimage.

THIRD MISSING PIECE
CHAUCER
THE MULTI-FACETED MEDIEVAL MAN

Whatever opinion scholars may have of *The Parson's Tale*, they seem to agree that it is quite different from all the other tales. It is in prose. It is long, it is not fiction. Chaucer's own *Tale of Melibee* is also long and in prose, but fiction. Whether Chaucer intended to instruct or bore with that tale is open to question. It is a story about Melibius whose wife and daughter were beaten up by an intruder while he was out working. It presents the question whether Melibius should be vengeful or, as his wife Prudence advocates, forgiving. The point is seriously taken by the Host who wishes his own wife had some of Dame Prudence's qualities. But the reader wonders if Chaucer, who has just failed to entertain with the *Tale of Sir Topas*, is still teasingly pretending to be a very dull, unaccomplished story teller.

The Parson's Tale, on the other hand, seems perfectly suited to its teller, and that teller is one Chaucer has admired without reserve. It is not fiction, as the Parson makes very clear. It is based on three treatises of theological scholars but transposed into the voice of a simple, sincere country parish priest who sometimes strays from the points he has planned, numerically, but rarely indulges in rhetoric. Now the reader must wonder again what was in Chaucer's mind as he transposed this material. Nowhere does he seem to be jesting or having the Parson take it lightly. (13) He is not without wit and satire, but his satire is reserved for some contemporary fashions in dress, speech, and behavior. Never does Chaucer indicate doubt about the Parson's sincerity or devotion to God. So sincere is he that, as the Tale progresses, the voice of Chaucer himself seems to blend with that of the Parson.

What do we learn here of Chaucer from the voice of the Parson?

First that Chaucer was a religious man; not sentimentally religious, but rather realistically so. He did not regard Jesus Christ as a "buddy," nor even as a wise teacher. He saw Him as Almighty God Incarnate before whom men should kneel in loving reverence. He regarded the Church Christ founded as the way given to men to reach everlasting life in heaven. He regarded men as sinful creatures yet worthy of great respect and dignity, created by God for eternal life. The only time he allows the Parson to shade contempt for the sin with contempt for the sinner is in speaking of clergy unfaithful to their high calling. He regarded the prophets of the Old Testament and the Fathers of the New as speakers of clear, understandable Truth. Life was a mixture of sorrow and joy, ups and downs, at times amusing, always interesting, never boring. Finally, he regarded himself as as another sinner among many, no better, no worse, but with the need for grace.

Another aspect of the voice of Chaucer slipping into the voice of the the Parson, deliberately or not, we never know, is in the imagery. Although the prose, seriousness of the subject, and the address to the intellect may be thought to make this tale remote from the other tales, it contains several colorful similes and images that are recognizable as Chaucer's tongue-in-cheek satire. For example, in the explanation on Pride in dress, he compares the buttocks of a man addicted to short shirts and tight hose which show off his posterior to "the hind end of a she-ape in the full of the moon, full horrible to see." A bit further on he adds, "For certainly from that part of their body they purge their stinking odor, they show to people proudly" He has a few things to say about the same short shirts over parti-colored hose which made half their "private members" which protrude red and white or blue and white or black and white as if "corrupted by the fire of St. Anthony or cancer or other such mischance." Exterior pride, he notes, is a sign of interior pride as the "gay bush at a tavern door is a sign of the wine that is in the cellar."

He compares envy to a blacksmith who "holds a hot iron to the heart of a man with a pair of long tongs of "longe rancor." He compares lecherous old men to a dog who "comes to the rose bush or other bush and lifts his leg though he cannot piss, but he holds his leg up to make a pretence to piss." He warns the good and chaste to avoid bad company for a white wall may be blackened by a candle, though it may not catch fire itself. He compares mortal and venial sin to the sinking of a ship. The ship may sink fast in a terrible storm or slowly through a leak in the sink in the hold of the ship. Either way, it ends up on the bottom.

He wryly says the man who does no good works should sing the new French song, "*Jay tout perdu mon temp et mon labour.*"

Other times when the voice of the narrator seems to be that of Chaucer himself are in places the voice is hesitant; for example, in speaking of sins of pride that we slip into without conscious intent, he notes that these may be grievious, "But I gesse that they ne been nat deedly." He apologizes for not discussing the Ten Commandments: "But so huge a doctrine I lete to the divines*" even though, as he notes, he has touched on them all. Although he has quoted from the Old and New Testaments and the Fathers (14), especially Saint Augustine, it is clear Chaucer does not consider himself or his Parson a theologian or a "divine," by any means.

But never can one say that the voice of the Tale does not seem well suited to the characterization of the Parson who speaks with the authority vested in his sacramental role. He emphasizes this authority with frequent use of "For certes," "soothly," "it is sooth," "truly" and many, many quotes from the

Fathers of the Church and the Bible. He has much to say about sex and methods of abortion and contraception which make one realize there is nothing new under the sun. The one sin he says is too horrible for him to even name is, apparently, sodomy* which he notes Holy Scripture can name and does; but Scripture is like the sun that can shine on the dung hill without becoming corrupted.

There are a few moments of dramatic rhetoric seeming to be of both voices. There is the description of the pains of hell for the proud, which calls to mind Dante's *Inferno*. Then there are the closing lines of the *Tale*, mentioned earlier, which poetically describe the "blisse of heaven."

Then come the *Retractions*. This, of course, is the voice of Chaucer alone, but, after *The Parson's* Tale, it seems to have the benediction of the Parson. It is a key part of the whole process of Penitence, Chaucer's own Penitence. It brings a closure not only to *The Parson's Tale* and *The Canterbury Tales* but also to Chaucer's own literary life.

For many centuries there has been a practice among Christians referred to as an **Examination of Conscience,*** done with a certain regularity --- daily by some, or weekly, monthly or at least yearly by the less motivated. It seems as if the study and transposition of these treatises on penitence and sin might have been a strong and effective Examination of Conscience for Chaucer, himself. It has been that for more than one reader. To what use have we put the time and talent God gave us ? As we ponder this from the medieval point of view, the reason for the *Retractions* becomes clear and we gain insight into the very loveable heart of Chaucer himself. True humility ts a lovely attribute. We ourselves can acknowledge how hard it is to accept any rebuke, especially such a solemn one that holds a mirror up to our soul; it would be pleasanter to disclaim all guilt for our transgressions. Here, Chaucer accepts a very harsh rebuke from himself. For our part, we are reluctant to see him retract because in some way, his retraction implicates us. For this reason we can see why *The Parson's Tale* and the *Retractions* are not Chaucer's most popular works.

The assumptions I have made about Chaucer's reaction to his work on *The Parson's Tale* must remain pure speculation, of course. We know little more about his life than we know about Shakespeare's. The *Retractions* is the only thing that comes close to a personal letter. There is no evidence that his literary genius was recognized or rewarded monetarily. It is not even certain when any of his writings were done. *The Book of the Duchess,* a memorial for John of Gaunt's (15) second wife is the first work for which a date, can be supposed, 1369, since that is the year she died. Scholars speculate that most of his writing was done after that period. *The Canterbury Tales* was probably written between 1380 and his death in 1400, and the pilgrimage is thought to have taken place on or about April 16, 1387 (16). Whether Chaucer himself ever actually took such a pilgrimage is not clear, but many think it probable.

CHAUCER'S LIFE

Chaucer' life was spent in the service of the court over the reigns of three kings: Edward III, Richard II, and Henry IV (17). Most of the records we have of him concern payments made for services to the Crown. (18) It is apparent from these that he rose in service from a page in the household of Lionel, the Duke of Clarence, son of Edward III, to envoy between the King and the Duke stationed in Calais*, to squire in the King's own household. The "vallettus" or "esquire "that was his office can be compared to what we would call a secretary in charge of important messages and secret service work, as well as supervision of property.

We know he was the supervisor of construction on various public buildings including the Tower of London and St. George's Chapel, Westminister, and some royal residences. We know he served in Flanders, France, and briefly in Italy where he might have met Boccaccio and Petrarch. He was Controller of Customs for the Port of London from 1374 until 1386 when he became Justice of the Peace for Kent and then Knight of the Shire, and thus a member of Parliament.

He had married Philippa Roet, a Lady of the Chamber to the Queen Philippa, wife of Edward III, in the 1360's. Chaucer's wife was sister to the third wife of John of Gaunt, and received her own pension from the crown. They had one son, Thomas who became chief butler to King Richard II, and probably another "litel sone Lowys" for whom he wrote *A Treatise on the Astrolabe*. No record gives us knowledge of other children. Philippa died about 1387.

We know some of his friends and associates: John Gower, an English poet who was put in charge of his affairs when he left for France; Ralph Strode, a Fellow of Merton College at Oxford; Eustache Deschamps, a contemporary of Chaucer and a popular poet in the French court, who sent him a copy of his poems with a ballad dedicated to the "Grant translateur, noble Geffroy Chaucer." There is further evidence of other friends who were noblemen and literary men.

From studying his sources, scholars have concluded that, like a gentleman of his age, he knew Latin, French and Italian, but probably not Greek. He translated the thirteenth century allegorical French love poem *Le Roman de la Rose* and the sixth century *Consolations of Philosophy* of Boethius. These are thought to have had a strong influence on him and his work. The influence of Boccaccio is found in *The Knight's Tale*, *Troilus and Criseyde* and the story of the patient Griselda of *The Clerk's Tale* which he took from Petrarch's translation into Latin of Boccaccio's *Decameron*. Dante, too, appears in the *Invocation* of *The Second Nun's Tale* and the *Troilus*.

What do we know of the man from this bit of information ? Most of his life seems to have been spent in service to the court; he was well read: he enjoyed the poetry and romances popular in that day as well as the religious tracts, the *Bible*, and the works of the Doctors of the Church. This was not uncommon knowledge to the medieval man. We know that the King and his court must have found him dependable and intelligent, a good writer and communicator or he would probably not have risen to such responsible positions.

Some would assume that his literary career was an avocation rather than his primary interest. That, again, must be speculation. Certainly *The Canterbury Tales* do not appear to have been prepared with the idea of presentation to the public close at hand. Nevertheless, they seem to tell us more about Chaucer the literary genius than any other work, to some degree because of their variety and to some degree because he includes himself as one of the characters. Since they are, for us today, the primary source of our understanding of the man, it is all the more pity to exclude the last tale and denigrate his final words.

It is true that there are scholars who never once had a twinkle in their eye; there are religious people so myopic they cannot focus on the greatness and goodness of God; there are satirists who become frostbitten; there are politicians who become betrayers; there are lovers of romance who never come down to earth; there are earthy jokesters who never come up for air; there are poets who always sing to the same tune. And then, on the other hand, there is **Chaucer**.

And so I bring this introduction to a close and hope that you will find the following version easy to follow, interesting, and thought-provoking. My objective was to make it faithful to Chaucer but clear to that modern reader who finds Middle English a stumbling block. The divisions in the Prologue and those in the text (some with English sub-headings in CAPITAL LETTERS) are mine because Chaucer's pattern of page-long paragraphs is unappealing to the modern reader. The Latin sub-headings are from the original Robinson text, probably taken from the Ellesmere Manuscript* (conserved at the noted Huntington Library, San Marino, California) which Professor Robinson judged to be the best of the early manuscripts (19).

Mary Farrell Pomerleau
Kettering, Ohio
March 25 , 1995

The Parson

The Prologue of the Parson's Tale

By that the Manciple had his tale ended,
The sun from the south line was descended,
So low that he was not, to my sight,
Nine degrees and twenty, as to height,
Four o'clock it was, I guess,
Eleven foot, a little more more or less,
Was my shadow at this time there
As the same feet as if my length were
Parted in six feet of equal portion.
Therewith the moon's exaltation
I mean Libra was ascending
As we were a village entering,
Our host began, as was his way,
To direct our jolly company,

 Said this: "Lords each and everyone,
Now we lack no more tales than one,
Fulfilled is my sentence and my decree,
I trust we have heard from each degree.
Almost fulfilled is all my plan,
I pray God give good luck to the man
That tells this tale to us lustily.

 "Sir priest," said he "are you a vicar ?
Or are you a parson ? Tell truth, by your faith,
Be what you art, you'll break not our fun
Every man but you has told his tale,
Unbuckle and show us what's in your bag,
For truly I think by your complexion
You could come up with a great fiction.
Tell us a story, for cockle bones!"
 The parson answered all at once

"You'll get no fable told by me,
For Paul writes unto Timothy,
'Reprove those who forsake truth
And tell fables and such wretchedness,'
Why should I sow chaff out of my fist,
When I could sow wheat, if I so list ?
For which I say if you wish to hear
Moralities and virtuous matter
And then you would give me audience
I would faithfully, with Christian reverence
Do you permissable kindness, as I can.
But know well, I am a southern man,
I can't recite 'rum, ram ruf' by letter
Nor, God knows, make rhyme little better;

And therefore, if you listen --- I will not gloss
--- I will tell you a merry* tale in prose
To knit up all these feats and make an end.
And Jesus, by his grace, wit me send
To show you the way, on this voyage,
To a perfect glorious pilgrimage
That promises the Jerusalem celestial.
And if you permit, at once I shall
Begin my tale, for which I pray
Reckon your opinion, I can no better say.
But nevertheless, this meditation
I place it ever under correction
Of clerks*, for I am not well-read
I take but the sentence*, well-trusted.
Therefore I make a protestation
That I will abide by correction."

  Upon this word we assented to
For as it seemed it was right to do
To end with some virtuous sentence
And to give him space and audience;

And bade our host to to him say
That to tell his tale we all him pray.

Our host had the words for us all:
"Sir priest," quoth he,"now good to you fall!
Tell," said he," your meditation.
But hurry, the sun will be down;
Be fruitful, and take little space,
And do well, God send you his grace!
Say what thou wish, and we will gladly hear."
And with that word he spoke in this manner.

Explicit prohemium
The prologue ends.

THE PARSON'S TALE

Jeremiah 6:16 " Thus says the Lord: Stand beside the earliest roads, ask the pathways of old which is the way to good, and walk it; thus you will find rest for your souls."

Our sweet Lord of Heaven who wishes no man would perish but wishes that we would come to the knowledge of Him and to the blissful life that is eternal, advises us through the Prophet Jeremiah* who says thus: Stick to the way and stand up and search out of old judgements which is the good way and walk in that way and you will find refreshment for your souls. Many are the spiritual ways that lead people to Our Lord Jesus Christ and to the reign of glory. Of these ways there is a truly noble and fitting way which will not fail for a man or woman who through sin has left the right way to the heavenly Jerusalem; this way is called Penitence, which man should gladly consider and weigh with all his heart.

PENITENCE

What is Penitence and why is it called Penitence and how many ways are there to do penitential acts, and which things pertain to penance and which things prevent it.

Saint Ambrose* said that Penitence is the satisfaction of man for the sin that he has done and should do no more. And some doctor says, " Penitence is the lamenting of man that has sorrow for his sins and grieves himself for what he has done wrong." Penitence, in certain circumstances, is the sincere repentance of a man who restrains himself in sadness and pain for his sins. And if he is truly penitent, he shall first confess the sins that he has done and steadfastly determine in his heart to go to confession, to do penance, and never to do things for which he ought to bewail or lament, and to continue in good works, or else his repentance is to no avail. For as Saint Isadore* says: "He is a joker and liar and no true penitent who immediately does again the thing for which he should repent." Weeping and not stopping the doing of sin may not avail. But nevertheless, men shall hope that every time a man falls, be it ever so often, he may rise through penance, if he has grace, but certainly that is doubtful. For as Saint Gregory* says, "with difficulty he rises out of his sin who is used to evil actions." And therefore, repentant people who refrain from sin and abandon sin before that sin controls them, holy church holds them sure of their salvation. And he that sins and truly repents at his last end, holy church still hopes for his salvation, by the great mercy of Our Lord Jesus Christ, because of his repentance; but take the surer way.

And now, since I have explained to you what Penitence is, now you should understand that there are three actions of Penitence. The first is that a man be

baptized after he has sinned. For Saint Augustine*
says, "Unless he be sorry for his old sinful life, he
may not begin his new life clean." For certainly, if he
be baptized without sorrow for his old sins, he
receives the mark of baptism, but not the grace nor the
remission of his sins until he has true repentance.
Another defect is this, that men do mortal sins after
they have received baptism. The third defect is that
men fall into venial sins after their baptism, from day
to day. Therefore, Saint Augustine* says that the peni-
tence of good and humble folk is the penitence of
every day.

The kinds of Penitence are three. One is formal and
public, another is common, and the third is private.
The penance that is formal is of two kinds; for ex-
ample, to be put out of holy church in Lent for the
slaughter of children and such manner of things. An-
other is when a man has sinned openly and it is infa-
mous and spoken of openly in the country. Then holy
church constrains him to do public penance. Common
or ordinary penance is that done when priests encour-
age men, in certain cases perhaps, to go on pilgrim-
ages without clothes or barefoot. Private penance is
that which a man does at any time after private con-
fession for which he receives private penance.

Now you shall understand what is profitable and
necessary for truly perfect Penitence. This rests on
three things: contrition of heart, confession of mouth,
and satisfaction. Saint John Chrysostom* says: "Peni-
tence constrains a man to accept kindly every pain that
is given him with contrition of heart and confession
of mouth and satisfaction; and in working in all humi-
lity." And this is fruitful Penitence against three things
in which we anger Our Lord Jesus Christ: this is to say
by lust in thinking, by recklessness in speaking, and
by wicked sinfulness in working. And against these
wicked sins is Penitence that may be likened to a tree.

CONTRITION OF HEART

The root of this tree is contrition that hides itself in the heart of him who is truly repentant just as the root of a tree hides itself in the earth. From the root of contrition springs a stalk that bears branches and leaves of confession and fruit of satisfaction. For which Christ says in His Gospel, "Do worthily the fruit of Penitence," for by this fruit may men know this tree and not by the root that is hid in the heart of man, nor by the branches nor the leaves of confession And therefore, Our Lord Jesus Christ says: "By their fruit shall you know them."

From this root also springs a seed of grace which is the mother of purity and this seed is sharp and fervent. The grace of this seed springs from God through remembrance of the day of doom and the pains of hell. Of this matter, Solomon* says that in the fear of God, man abandons his sin. The passion of this seed is the love of God and the desire for the joys of eternity. This passion draws the heart of a man to God and makes him hate his sin. For truly, there is nothing which tastes so good to a child as the milk of his nurse and nothing is more hateful to him than this milk when it is mixed with other food. Just so, the sinful man that loves his sin, to him it seems the sweetest of all things but from that time he loves steadily Our Lord Jesus Christ and desires eternity, then there is to him nothing more abominable. For truly, the law of God is the love of God; as David the prophet says: " I have loved thy law and hated wickedness and hate." He that loves God keeps His word and His law. This is the tree the prophet Daniel * saw in spirit when after the dream of King Nebuchadnezzar*, he advised him to do penance. Penance is the tree of life to them that receive it and he that holds to true penitence is blessed after the word of Solomon.

In this penitence or contrition, man shall under-
stand four things; what is contrition and what are the
causes that move a man to contrition; how should he
be contrite and what does contrition do for the soul. It
is thus: contrition is the very sorrow that a man
receives in his heart for his sins with firm purpose to
go to confession and do penance and never more to
sin. And this is the manner of this sorrow according
to Saint Bernard*: " He shall be heavy and grievous
and fully sharp and poignant in his heart." First
because the man has offended his Lord and Creator,
and more poignant because he has offended his Fa-
ther in Heaven; and yet more sorrowing because he
has angered and offended Him that bought him and
with His precious Blood has delivered us from the
bonds of sin, and from the cruelty of the devil and
from the pains of hell.

SIX CAUSES TO MOVE MAN TO CONTRITION

The causes that ought to move a man to contrition
are six. First a man ought to think about his sins, but
this thinking should not give him delight but great
shame and sorrow. For Job says: "Sinful men do
works worthy of confession." And therefore, says
Ezekiel,* "I will remember all the years of my life in
the bitterness of my heart." And God says in the
Apocalypse*, "Remember from whence you are fallen,
for before the time you sinned, you were the children
of God and the participants in the kingdom of God,
but for your sins you have become the slaves of the
fiend, the enemy of the angels, the scandal of holy
church, and the food of the false serpent, perpetual
matter for the fires of hell, yet more foul and abo-
minable for you have trespassed so often as does the
dog that returns to eat his spewing. And yet you are
fouler for your long continuance in sin and sinful

usage for which you are as rotten in your sin as a beast in his dung. Such manner of thoughts make a man ashamed of his sin and it gives him no pleasure as God says through the prophet Ezekiel, "You shall remember your ways and they shall displease you." Truly sin is the way that leads people to hell.

The second cause that ought to make a man hate sin is this; as Saint Peter* says, "Whoever does sin is the slave of sin." Sin puts a man in great slavery. And, therefore, the prophet Ezekiel says, "I went sorrowfully, in disdain for myself." Certainly a man ought to have disdain for sin and leave that thraldom and villainy. And what does Seneca* say in this matter ? He says this: "Though I thought that neither God nor man may know of it, yet would I disdain to commit sin." And the same Seneca also said, "I am born to greater things than to be a slave to my body, or to make of my body a slave." No fouler slavery may no man nor woman make of his body than to give his body to sin. Although it were the foulest churl or the foulest woman that lives and of the least value, yet is he that sins more foul and more in servitude. Always, from the higher degree a man falls, the more enslaved he is and the more vile and abominable he is to God and to the world. O Good God, a man should do well to have disdain for sin since before sin he was free and now he is in bondage. And, therefore, Saint Augustine says, "If you have disdain for your servant because he offends or sins, then you should have disdain for yourself if you should sin." Take stock of your value that you do not become foul to yourself.

Alas! They ought to be ashamed of themselves and hate having been the servants and slaves of sin whom God in His endless goodness has raised to a high estate, given him intelligence, a strong body, health, beauty, prosperity and bought him from death with

His heart's blood, who so unkindly, against His gentleness, left Him so villainously to slaughter their own souls. O Good God, you women of great beauty, remember the proverbs of Solomon. He said "Consider a woman that is a fool with her body like a ring of gold that is in the snout of a sow." For just as a sow tears about with the snout in all kinds of filth, so she roots her beauty in the stinking filth of sin.

THE PAINS OF HELL

The third cause that should move a man to contrition is dread of the day of doom and of the horrible pains of hell. For, as Saint Jerome says, "Every time I remember the day of doom, I quake; for when I eat or drink or whatever I do, it seems to me the trumpet sounds in my ear: 'Rise up. you that have been dead and come to the judgement.'" O Good God, a man ought to dread such a judgement. "There we shall all be," as Saint Paul* says, "before the seat of Our Lord Jesus Christ," where He shall make a general congregation where no man may be absent. For certainly, there no excuses will avail. And not only our faults shall be judged but also all our works shall be known. And as Saint Bernard says, "There no pleading shall prevail; no tricks; we shall give reckoning of every idle word." There we shall have a judge that may not be deceived or corrupted. Why ? Certainly all our thoughts have been revealed to him; not for prayer, not for reward shall He be corrupted. And therefore Solomon says, "The wrath of God will not be spared any creature for pleading or for gifts." And therefore, on the day of doom, no one may hope to escape. As Saint Anselm* says, "Very great anguish shall the sinful people have at that time. The stern and angry judge shall sit above, and under Him, the horrible pit of hell will be open to destroy them whose sins must now be known, which sins have been openly shown before

God and before every creature; and on the left side, more devils than can be imagined to harrass and draw sinful souls to the pains of hell, and within the hearts of people shall be the biting of conscience, and without shall be the world all burning up. Where then shall the wretched man flee to hide himself ? Certainly he may not hide; he must come forth and show himself. "For certainly," as Saint Jerome* says, "the earth shall cast him out and the sea also, and the air also that shall be full of thunder and lightning." Now, truly, whoever will remember these things, I guess his sin will not give him pleasure but rather great sorrow for fear of the pains of hell.

And therefore, Job* said to God, "Allow, Lord, that I may wail and weep awhile before I go without return into the dark land, covered with the darkness of death, to the land of misery and darkness, where is the shadow of death, where there is no order or law, but grisly fears that will last forever." Lo, here you may see that Job stayed in prayer a little while to weep and wail over his trespasses, for, truly, one day of respite is better than all the treasures of this world. And in as much as man may acquit himself before God by penitence in this world and not by treasure, he should pray to God to give him respite to weep and wail over his trespasses. For certainly all the sorrow that a man might have from the beginning of the world is but a little thing compared to the sorrow of hell.

Here is the reason Job called hell the land of darkness: understand he called it "land" or "earth" for it is stable and never shall pass away; "dark" for he that is in hell has no light of any kind. For certainly, the dark light that shall come out of the fire that shall burn forever shall turn him all to pain that is in hell, for it shows him to the horrible devils that shall torment him. "Covered with the darkness of death," that is to say that he that is in hell shall have lack of the sight of

God; for surely the sight of God is life eternal. "The darkness of death" is the sin that the wretched man has done, which prevents him from seeing the face of God, just as would a dark cloud between us and the sun.

"Land of misery." because there are three faults, three things that people of this world have in this present life, honors, pleasures, and riches. Instead of honors, in hell they have shame and confusion. For you know well that men call honor the reverence that man gives to man, but in hell there is neither honor nor reverence. For certain no more honor shall be given there to a king than to a knave. As God says through the prophet Jeremiah, "Those people that despise me shall be despised." Honor is also called the chief ruler; there shall be no creature serving others but to harm and torment.

Honor is also called great dignity and highness but in hell they shall all be trodden by devils. And God says, "The horrible devils shall come and go upon the rulers of the damned people." The higher they were in the present life, the lower shall they be in hell.

Instead of the riches of this world, they shall have the misery of poverty and this poverty shall be in four things: in lack of treasure, for David says, "The rich people that embraced and gave all their heart to the treasures of this world shall sleep the sleep of death and nothing shall they find in their hands of their treasure." And, moreover, the misery of hell shall be without meat or drink. For God says through Moses*: "They shall be wasted with hunger and the birds of hell shall devour them with sharp teeth and the gall of the dragon shall be their drink and the venom of the dragon their food." And their further misery shall be in a lack of clothing, for they shall be naked except for the fire in which they burn, and other filth. And they shall be naked of soul, without any virtues which are the clothing of the soul. Where then will be the beautiful clothes, the soft sheets, the thin shirts. See what God says of them through the prophet Isaiah*: "Under them shall be strewn moths and their covering shall be the worms of hell."

And furthermore, their misery shall be in lack of friends. For he is not poor who has good friends, but there is no friend, for neither God nor any creature shall be a friend to him, and each one of them shall hate the others with a deadly hate. "The sons and the daughters shall rebel against their fathers and mothers and kindred against kindred and chide and despise each other day and night," as God says through the prophet Micah*. And the loving children, those who loved each other in the flesh will each eat the other if they could. For how should they love each other in the pains of hell when they hated each other in this life ? For know this fleshly love was deadly hate, as the prophet David says: "Whosoever loves wickedness hates his soul." And, whosoever hates his own soul, certainly in no way loves any other creature. And therefore, in hell is no comfort, no friendship but always the more carnal the relationships that are in hell, the more cursing and deadly hatred there is among them. •

And furthermore, they shall be without any kind of pleasures. For certain the pleasures of the five senses: sight, hearing, smelling, tasting, and touching. In hell their sight shall be full of darkness and smoke and therefore tears; and their hearing full of moaning and the grinding of teeth, as Jesus Christ says. Their nostrils shall be full of stinking odors, and as Isaiah the prophet says,"their taste shall be full of bitter gall." And "touching their bodies all over, a fire that will never be quenched, and worms that will never die," as God said by the mouth of Isaiah. And in so far that they should not doubt that they may die in pain and by their death flee from pain, there are the words of Job, "there as the shadow of death." Certainly a shadow has the likeness of the thing of which it is the shadow but the shadow is not the same as the thing. So it is with the pain of hell; it is like death for the horrible anguish. And why ? Because it pains them forever as though they should die again, but they will certainly not die. As Saint Gregory says, "To the wretched captives there shall be death without death and end without end and losses without ever ceasing." For their death shall always live and their end shall always be beginning and their losses shall last. Saint John the Evangelist* says, "They shall follow death and shall not find him; they shall desire to die and death shall flee from them."

And Job says that in hell there is no order or law. God has created all things with the right order and nothing without order but all things have been ordered and numbered; yet they that have been damned find nothing in order nor keep any order. For the earth shall bear them no fruit. As the prophet David says, "God shall destroy the fruit of the earth for them; water shall give them no moisture, nor the air any refreshment, nor the fire any light." As Saint Basil* says, "The burning of the fire of this world shall God give in hell to them that are damned, but the light and the clarity shall be given to His children in Heaven," just as the good man gives meat to his children. and bones to his hounds. They shall have no hope of escape says Saint Job, "there shall horror and grisly dread dwell without end." Horror is always to fear the harm that is to come and this fear shall always be in the hearts of those who have been damned.

They have lost all hope for seven reasons. First because God who is their judge shall be without mercy on them; and they may not please Him nor any of His saints; and they may give nothing for their ransom;

they have no voice to speak to Him; they may not flee from pain. They have no goodness in them that they might show to deliver themselves from pain. And, therefore, Solomon says: "The wicked man dies and when he is dead, he shall have no hope of escaping from pain." Whoever then understands these pains well and realizes that he deserves these pains for his sins certainly should have more appetite to mourn and weep than to sing and play. As to that, Solomon says: "Whoever has the wisdom to know the pains that are established and ordained for sin would be sorrowful." "This wisdom," says Saint Augustine, "makes a man lament in his heart."

The fourth point that ought to make a man contrite is the sad remembrance of the good that he left undone on earth and also the good he has lost. Surely he has lost the good works, whether they are the good works he did before he fell into mortal sin or the good works he did while he lay in sin. Truly, the good works he did before he fell into sin have been deadened and confounded and dulled by frequent sinning. The other good works that he did while in mortal sin, they are utterly useless for the life of eternity in Heaven. Then these good works that have been deadened by sinning, which good works he did while he was in charity, shall never live again without true penitence. And, therefore, God says through the mouth of Ezekiel, "If the just man turns from his just ways and works wickedness, shall he live?" No, for all the good works he has done shall never be remembered for he shall die in his sin. And Saint Gregory says thus on this subject: "We shall understand this first, that when we commit mortal sin, it is useless then to rehearse or point to the good works we have done before." For surely, in the doing of the mortal sin, there is no security in any good work we have done before, that is to say, as far as having by that, eternal life in heaven.

But, nevertheless, the good works live again and come again and help us to eternal life in heaven when we have contrition. But truly, the good works that men do while in mortal sin, in as much as they were in deadly sin, never live again. For certainly, things that never had life may never live. Nevertheless, although they never help one to have life eternal, yet they help alleviate the pain of hell or else help to get temporal riches, or else help that God will illumine the heart of sinful man to repent; and they also help a man to become accustomed to doing good works so the fiend has less power over his soul. And thus the gracious Lord Jesus Christ wishes that no good work be lost, for in some way it will avail. But, in as much as the good works a man does while in the good life are ruined by committing sin afterwards, and also since all the good works that men do while they are in mortal sin are already dead as far as eternal life goes, a man that does no good work could sing this new French song," *Jay tout perdu mon temps et mon labour."*

For certainly sin bereaves a man of both the goodness of nature and the goodness of grace. Truly, the grace of the Holy Ghost travels like fire that may not be idle; for fire fails as soon as it has finished its work and grace fails as soon as it finishes its work. Then the sinful man loses the glory that is only bestowed on good men that labor and work. He may well be sorry then who owes his life to God as long as he lives that he has no goodness to pay his debt to God to whom he owes his life. For trust well, "he shall give an account,"as Saint Bernard says, "of all the goods that he has been given in this present life and how he has spent them; there shall not be a hair of his head, nor a moment of an hour of his lifetime that will perish without his giving a reckoning of it."

THE SUFFERINGS OF CHRIST

The fifth thing that ought to move a man to contrition is the memory of the passion Our Lord Jesus Christ suffered for our sins. As Saint Bernard says, "While I live I shall remember the travails that Our Lord Jesus Christ suffered in preaching, his weariness in suffering, his temptations when he fasted, his long waking when he prayed, his tears when he wept in pity for good people, the woe, and the shame and the filth that men said to him, the foul spitting that men spat in his face, the blows that men gave him, the foul words and reproofs that men said to him, the nails with which he was nailed to the cross, and all that he suffered for my sins and nothing for his guilt." And you should understand that in man's sin, every manner of law and order is turned upsidedown. For it is true that God and reason and emotions and the body of man have been so ordered that each of these four things should have lordship over the next; God should have lordship over reason, and reason over the emotions, and emotions over the body of man. But truly, when a man sins, all this order is turned upsidedown and, therefore, in as much as the reason of man will not be subject to God who is his Lord by right, it loses the dominion it should have over the emotions and the body of man. Why ? Emotion rebels against reason and that way reason loses the control over sensuality and the body. Just as reason rebels against God, emotion rebels against reason and the body also. And this disorder and rebellion Our Lord Jesus Christ paid for very dearly with his precious body, and listen to the way.

In as much as reason is rebellious to God, man is worthy to have sorrow and be dead. This Our Lord Jesus Christ suffered for man after he had been betrayed by his disciple, taken and bound so that blood burst out at every nail in his hands, as Saint Augustine says. And more, as much as the reason of man will not control emotion when it may, man should be shamed, and this Our Lord Jesus Christ suffered for man when they spit on his face. And furthermore, as much as the wretched body of man is rebel to both reason and emotion, it is worthy of death. And this Our Lord Jesus Christ suffered for man on the cross where there was no part of his body without pain and bitter passion. And this Jesus Christ suffered who never did wrong. And, therefore, it may reasonably be said of Jesus, "Too much am I pained for the things that I never deserved and too much disgraced for shame that man is worthy to have." And therefore, the sinful man might well say, as says Saint Bernard, "Accursed be the bitterness of my sin for which must be suffered so much bitterness." For certainly, in the diverse disagreements of our wickedness, the passion of Jesus Christ was ordered in diverse things.

It is thus: sinful man's soul is betrayed by the devil through greed for temporal prosperity or tricked when he chooses pleasures of the flesh; it is tormented by impatience in adversity and beset by servitude and subjection to sin, at last is finally slain For this disorder in sinful man, Jesus Christ was first betrayed and after that was bound; that was to unbind us from sin and pain. Then he was scorned who should only have been honored in all things and above all things. Then his face which all mankind ought to desire to see and which the angels desire to see was vilely spat upon.Then he was scourged,who had done no wrong. Finally, he was crucified and slain.Then the word of Isaiah was accomplished: "He was wounded for our misdeeds and defiled for our offenses." Now since Jesus Christ took upon himself the pain of all our wickedness, sinful man should weep and wail much that God's son of heaven should endure all this pain.

The sixth thing that ought to move a man to contrition is the hope of three things: forgiveness of sins, the gift of grace to do well, and the glory of heaven with which God shall reward man for his good deeds. And in as much as Jesus Christ gives us these gifts from his largesse* and his sovereign bounty, he is called *Jhesus Nazarenus, Rex Judeorum. Jhesus* is to say *saveour* or *salvacion,* on whom men should hope to have forgiveness of sins which is properly salvtion from sins. And, therefore, the angel said to Joseph, "Thou shall call his name Jesus, who shall save his people from their sins." And Saint Peter says, "There is no other name under heaven that is given to any man by which a man may be saved but only Jesus." *Nazarenus* is as much as to say *florishing* in which a man shall hope that he who gives him remission of sins shall also give him the grace to do well. For in the flower is the hope of the fruit in time to come and in forgiveness of sin the hope of grace to do well. " I was at the door of your heart," said Jesus, "and called to enter. He that opens to me shall have forgiveness of sins. I will enter into him by my grace and sup with him" by the good works that he shall do, which works are the food of God; "and he shall sup with me," by the great joy that I shall give him. Thus shall man hope for his works of penance that God will give him his kingdom, as he promised him in the Gospel.

THE MANNER OF CONTRITION

Now a man should understand in what manner his contrition should be. I say it should be universal and total. That is to say a man should be truly repentant for all the sins that he has commited through the delight of his thoughts, for delight is full of danger. There are two manners of consenting: one is called consent of affection, when a man is moved to sin and it delights him for a long while to think of that sin, and his reason understands well that it is a sin against the law of God, and yet his reason does not restrain his foul delight or desire, though he perceives well that it is against reverence for God. Though his reason might not consent to do that sin in deed, yet, some doctors say, that such desire for a long while is very perilous, though it be ever so little. A man should have sorrow for all that he ever desired against the law of God with full consent of his reason, for there is no doubt that there is mortal sin in consenting. For certainly, there is no mortal sin that is not first in the thoughts and after that in his desire and then in his consent and then in the deed. Therefore, I say that many men are who never repent of such thoughts and desires, never shrive themselves of them but only of the the great sin of outward deed. Wherefore I say that such wicked thoughts and wicked desires are subtle beguilers of those who shall be damned.

Moreover, man ought to be sorry for his wicked words as well as his wicked deeds. For certainly to repent of a single sin and not of all his other sins or to repent of other sins and not a certain single sin will be to no avail. For certainly God Almighty is all good and therefore he forgives all, or else really nothing. Of this Saint Augustine says: "I know for certain God is the enemy of every sinner." How then can he that notes only one sin have forgiveness for the remainder of his sins ? No!

And furthermore, contrition should be truly sorrowful and sincere and, therefore, God gives him full mercy, and, therefore, when my soul was anguished within me, I had remembrance of God that my prayer might come to him. Furthermore, contrition must be continual that man may have the steadfast purpose to confess himself and amend his life. For truly, while contrition lasts, man may ever have hope of forgive-

ness; and from this comes a hatred of sin that destroys
sin both within himself and in other people who come
under his influence. As David says: "You that love
God hate wickedness." For trust well, to love God is
to love what he loves and hate what he hates.

THE PROFIT OF CONTRITION

The last thing man should understand about con-
trition is this: when does contrition avail ? I say that
sometimes contrition delivers a man from sin; as Da-
vid says, "I say," says David, that is to say I firmly
purpose, "to shrive me and thou, Lord, release me
from my sins." And just so, contrition avails nothing
without the firm purpose of confession if man have the
opportunity, even as confession or satisfaction is
worth little without contrition. And furthermore, con-
trition destroys the power of hell and makes weak and
feeble all the strengths of the devils, and restores the
gifts of the Holy Ghost, and all good virtues. It clean-
ses the soul of sin and delivers the soul from the pains
of hell and from the company of the devil and from the
servitude of sin and it restores all spiritual goods and
to the company and communion of holy church. It
makes him who was the son of wrath the son of grace.
All these things have been proved by holy scripture.
Therefore, he that would set his intentions on these
things is truly wise for truly, he should not then have
the courage to sin in his whole life, but rather give his
body and all his heart to the service of Our Lord Jesus
Christ and therefore do him homage. For truly, our
sweet Lord Jesus Christ has spared us so freely to our
follies that if he had not pity on man's soul, a sorry
song we might all sing.

Explicit prima pars Penitentie; Et sequitur secunda pars eiusdem.
The First Part of Penance Ends and the Second Part Follows.

CONFESSION

The second part of Penitence is confession; that is proof of contrition. Now you shall understand what confession is and whether it is necessary or not and what things are suitable to a valid (true) confession.

First you should understand confession is truly showing your sins to the priest. This is to say "truly," for a man must confess all the conditions that belong to his sin, as far as he can. And it must be said, nothing can be excused nor hidden nor covered up, and no boasting of your good works. And furthermore, it is necessary to understand from whence the sins sprang up, how they increased, and what they were..

ORIGINAL SIN

Of the springing up of sin, Saint Paul speaks in this manner: "just as through a man sin first entered into this world and through that sin death, just so this sin entered into all men that sinned." This man was Adam by whom all sin entered this world when he broke the commandments of God. Therefore, he that was so free that he would never die became one who must die whether he would or not, and all his progeny in this world that in this man sinned. Consider the state of innocence when Adam and Eve were naked in Paradise and had no shame of their nakedness. The serpent that was the most wily of all the beasts God made said to the woman, "Why does God command you not to eat of every tree in Paradise ?" The woman answered, "From the fruit of the trees in Paradise, we feed ourselves, but truly, of the fruit of the tree that is in the middle of Paradise, God has forbidden us to eat nor touch it, lest we die." The serpent said to the woman, "No, no, truly you shall not die for God knows that on that day you eat, your eyes shall be opened, and you shall be as gods, knowing good and evil." The woman then saw that the tree was good to eat, and fair to the eye and delightful to look upon. She took the fruit of the tree and ate it and gave it to her husband and he ate and the eyes of both were opened. And when they saw they were naked, they took fig leaves and sewed them like britches to cover their bodies.

There you may see that mortal sin first was at the suggestion of the devil, as shown here by the serpent, and next, the delight of the flesh as shown here by Eve, and after that the consenting of reason as shown here by Adam. For trust well, though the fiend tempted Eve, that is to say the flesh, and the flesh had delight in the beauty of the forbidden fruit, yet certainly until reason, that is to say Adam, consented to the eating of the fruit, he remained in the state of innocence.

From Adam we took original sin, for from his flesh, we all descended and inherited a vile and corrupt nature. And when the soul is put in our body, at once it contracts original sin and what was at first only the pain of concupiscence is afterwards both the pain and the sin. And therefore, we are all born sons of wrath and eternal damnation if we do not receive baptism which redeems us from the fault. But in truth, the pain lives with us as temptation which is chiefly concupiscence*. And concupiscence, when it is wrongly disposed in man, makes him covetous, covetous of the flesh, carnal sins, and covetous by the sight of his eyes for earthly things, and also covetous of honors by the pride of his heart.

CONCUPISCENCE

Now to speak of the first covetousness, concupiscence, in respect to our bodies that were made lawfully and by the right judgement of God. I say that in as much as man is not obedient to God who is his lord, his flesh is not obedient to him through concupiscence which is called the nourishment of sin and the occasion of sin. Therefore, all the while that man has within him the pain of concupiscence, it is impossible that he not be tempted sometimes and moved to sin. And this does not stop as long as he lives; it may well grow feeble and weak by virtue of baptism and by the grace of God through penance; but it shall never be fully quenched so that he will not sometime be tempted; if he were weakened by sickness, or some act of sorcery, or cold drinks. For consider what Saint Paul says: "The flesh fights against the spirit and the spirit against the flesh; they are so contrary and opposed that a man may not always do as he would." The same Saint Paul, after his great penances on water and on land --- in water by night and on land in great peril and great pain, on land in hunger and thirst, in cold and nakedness and once stoned almost to death, yet he said, "Alas, captive man, who shall deliver me from the prisons of my captive body ?" And Saint Jerome, after he had lived in the desert a long time with no company but wild beasts and no food or drink but herbs and water, yet said that "the fire of lechery boiled in his body." Therefore, I know for certain that they who say they have never been tempted in their body are deceived. Witness Saint James the Apostle who said, "every creature is tempted in his own concupiscence." That is to say that every one of us has matter and occasion to be tempted to the nourishing of sin that is in his body. Saint John the Evangelist says, "If we say we are without sin, we deceive ourselves and the truth is not in us."

CONSENT TO SIN

Now you should understand how sin grows or increases in man. The first thing is this nourishing of sin of which I spoke before, the fleshly concupiscence. And next comes the suggestion of the devil, that is to say the devil's bellows with which he blows the fire of fleshly concupiscence in man. And after that a man decides whether he will do the thing tempted or not. And then, if a man withstands the first enticement of the flesh and the fiend, then it is no sin. And if he does not do so, then at once he feels the flame of desire. And then it is good to beware and keep alert or else he will soon fall into consenting to sin; and then will he do it if he have the time and place. Moses quotes the devil in this manner: "The fiend says, 'I will chase and pursue man by wicked suggestions and I will catch him by the moving or stirring of sin. I will divide my prize or my victim within himself by deliberation and my wish will be accomplished in pleasure. I will draw my sword in consenting.' (For certainly just as a sword divides a thing in two, just so consenting divides God from man.) 'and then I will slay him in the death of sin,' thus says the fiend." For certainly then a man is quite dead in soul. Thus sin is accomplished by temptation, by desire, and by consenting; and then the sin is called actual.

MORTAL AND VENIAL SIN

In truth, sin is of two kinds: either it is venial or it is mortal sin. Truly, when a man loves any creature more than Jesus Christ, our Creator, it is deadly sin. And it is venial sin if a man loves Jesus Christ less than he ought. Truly, the act of this venial sin is very perilous for it diminishes the love men should have for God more and more. And if a man burden himself with many venial sins, but if he sometimes unburdens himself of them by confession, they will be less able to lessen the love of Jesus Christ in him. Venial sin slides into deadly sin. The more a man burdens his soul with venial sins, the more he is inclined to fall into deadly sin. And therefore, let us not be negligent in unburdening ourselves of venial sins. For the proverb says "many smalls make a great." And listen to this example. A great wave of the sea comes sometimes with such force that it drowns the ship. And the same harm is sometimes done by little drops of water that enter through a little crack in the sink in the ship's hull and through the bottom of the ship, if men are so negligent that they don't empty it in time. And though there is a difference between these two causes of drowning, either way the ship is drowned. Just so it sometimes is with mortal sin, and of annoying venial sins when they multiply so much that the worldly things that he loves, through which he sins venially, become as great in his heart as the love of God, or greater. And therefore, the love of everything that is not established in God, nor done principally for God's sake, although a man love it less than God, yet it is a venial sin, and deadly sin when anything weighs in his heart as much as the love of God, or more. "Deadly sin," as Saint Augustine says, "is when a man turns his heart from God who is the true, supreme, unchanging good and gives his heart to things that may change and pass away." And certainly, it is everything but the God of heaven. Certainly, if a man gives his love which he owes all to God, to a creature, as much of his love as he gives to this creature, that much he takes from God, and therefore he sins. For he that is in debt to God never repays all his debt, that is to say, all the love of his heart.

Now since man generally understands what venial sin is, then it is fitting to tell especially of sins which, perhaps, many a man does not deem sins and does not shrive himself of them, and yet, nevertheless, they are sins. Truly as the clerics have written, that is to say, that every time a man eats or drinks more than suffices to sustain his body, he certainly commits sin. And also when he speaks more than is needed, it is a sin. Also when he does not listen benignly to the complaints of the poor; also when he is in good health and will not fast when other folk fast, without reasonable cause; also when he sleeps more than he needs, or when because of this, he comes to church late, or to other works of charity; also when he uses his wife without the primary desire of procreation to the honor of God, or for the intention of yielding to his wife the debt of his body; also when he will not visit the sick and the prisoner, if he can; also if he love wife or child or other worldly thing more than reason requires; also if he flatters or fawns more than he ought for any reason; also if he wastes or withdraws the alms of the poor; also if he prepares his food more deliciously than is needed, or if he gobble it too greedily; also if he tell vain stories at church or at God's service, or if he is a speaker of idle words or villainy or folly, for he shall give an account of it on the day of doom. Also when he promises to do things that he may not perform; also when by jest or folly he calumniates or scorns his neighbor; also when he has any wicked suspicion of things he does not know to be true; these things and more without number are sins, as Saint Augustine says.

Now men shall understand that although no earthly man can escape all venial sins, yet he may refrain from them through the burning love he has for Our Lord Jesus Christ and by prayers and confession and other good works so that it shall aggravate him little.

For as Saint Augustine says, "If a man loves God in such a manner that all that he ever does is in the love of God and for the love of God, truly, for he burns with the love of God, it is like how much a drop of water that falls on a furnace of fire annoys or grieves, so much a venial sin annoys a man who is perfect in the love of Jesus Christ." Man may also remove venial sin by receiving worthily the precious body of Jesus Christ; also by using holy water; also by almsgiving; by general confession of the *Confiteor* at Mass and at Compline*, and by blessings of bishops and priests and other good works.

Explicit secunda pars Penitentie.
The Second Part of Penance Ends.

The Vice of Pride

THE SEVEN CAPITAL SINS

Sequitur de septem peccatis mortalibus et eorum dependenciis circumstanciis et speciebus
Here Follow the Seven Mortal Sins and Their Circumstances and Kinds

Now it is appropriate to tell what the seven deadly sins are, that is to say the chief sins. All of them are false but in different ways. Now they are called the chief sins in as much as they are the principal sins and all other sins spring from them. The root of these seven sins is **Pride**, the general root of all evil. For from this root spring certain branches such as **Anger**, **Envy**, **Sloth**, **Avarice** or Covetousness (commonly understood), **Gluttony** and **Lechery**. And every one of these chief sins has its branches and its twigs, as shall be shown in the following chapter.

PRIDE
De Superbia

Although no one can tell absolutely the number of twigs and the harm that comes from Pride, yet I shall show a part of them as you shall understand. There is Disobedience, Boasting, Hypocrisy, Spite, Arrogance, Impudence, Swelling of Heart, Elation, Strife, Impatience, Contumely, Presumption, Irreverence, Pertinacity, Vainglory and many other twigs that I cannot say.
Disobedience is in him who with scorn disobeys the commandments of God, and his sovereigns, and his spiritual father. **Boasting** is in a man bragging of the evil or the good that he has done. **Hypocrisy** is in man hiding what he is and showing himself as what he is not. **Spite** is in a man showing disdain for his neighbor, that is to say his fellow Christian, or despises doing what he ought to do.

Arrogance is in a man who thinks he has some virtues that he has not, or imagines that he deserves them, or else he thinks he is what he is not. **Impudence** is in a man who in his pride has no shame for his sins. **Swelling of heart** is in a man who rejoices in the harm that he has done. **Insolence** is in a man who despises in his judgment all other men, compared to his own value, his cunning, his speech, and his possessions. **Elation** is in one who cannot bear to have either a master or a companion. **Impatience** is in a man who will not be taught nor reproved for his faults and by contention opposes the truth with argument and defends his folly. **Contumely*** is in him who in his indignation is against every power or authority of those who are his sovereigns. **Presumption** is a man taking on an enterprise that he ought not to do or else that he cannot do, and this is called arrogance. **Irreverence** is present when men do not honor wherever as they ought and wait to be honored. **Pertinacity*** is present when man defends his folly and trusts too much in his own knowledge. **Vainglory*** is to have pomp and pleasure in his temporal greatness and glorify himself in this worldly estate. **Chattering** is to speak too much before people and chatter like a mill and take no heed to what they say.

And yet there is a private kind of pride in a man that waits first to be saluted before he will salute, even if he is of less worth than the other, perhaps, and also he seeks the occasion and desires to be situated or go before the other on the path, or the kiss of peace, or being incensed, or going to offering before his neighbor and such similar things, against his duty, perhaps, but he has his heart and his intention on such a proud desire to be magnified and honored before the people.

IMMODEST ATTIRE

Now there are two kinds of pride; one of them is within the heart of man and the other is without. The things I have just said and more pertain to the pride that is in the heart of man; the other kind of pride is without. Nevertheless, one of these kinds of pride is a sign of the other, just as the bright arbor or bush designating a tavern is a sign of the wine that is in the cellar. And this is the way in many things such as speech and countenance and in an outrageous array of clothing. For certainly if there were no sin in clothing, Christ would not have noted and spoken of the clothing of the rich man in the Gospel. Saint Gregory says, "Precious clothing is blamable for the lack of it, and for its softness and for its unusualness and design, and for the superfluity or scantiness of it." Alas! May men not see in our own days, the sinful, costly array of clothing, its too great superfluity, or its inordinate scantiness ?

As to the first sin, that is the excess of clothing which makes it so costly, to the harm of the people: not only the cost of embroidery the elaborate notching or barring with heraldry*, wavy lines, adorning with heraldic pales or stripes, entwining with heraldic bends and similar waste of cloth in vanity; but there is also costly fur on their gowns, so much punching with a chisel to make holes, so much cutting into peaks with shears; add to that the superfluity of length of the aforesaid gowns, trailing in the dung and the mire, on horse and on foot by men as well as women so that all this stuff trailing is truly in effect, wasted, consumed, threadbare, and rotten with dung, rather than being given to the poor, to the great damage to the aforesaid poor folk. And that is in many ways; that is to say, the more the cloth is wasted, the more it must cost people due to the scarcity. And furthermore, if it should be that they would give such punctured and slashed clothing to the poor folk, it would not be convenient for them to wear it in their state, nor suitable to their needs to keep them from the inclemency of the elements.

On the other hand, to speak of the lawless scantiness of clothing as these cut-off jackets or wretched things that because of their shortness do not cover the shameful members of a man; they show a wicked intention. Alas, some of them show the protuberance of their private parts and the horrible swollen members that seem like the malady of a hernia in the wrapping of their hose, and their buttocks appears like the hind part of a she-ape in the fullness of the moon. And moreover, the wretched, swollen members that they show through the new fashion in the separation of the hose to red and white, it seems as if half their shameful members had been scourged. And if it is that they wear their hose in other colors as white and black or white and blue or black and red and so forth, then it seems by the variety of color that half of their private parts were corrupted by the fire of Saint Anthony or by cancer, or by some other misfortune. The hind part of their buttocks is quite horrible to see. For certainly in that part of their body where they purge their stinking odor, that part they show to the people proudly in spite of dignity, that dignity that Jesus Christ and his friends observed and showed in their lives.

Now as to the outrageous array of women, God knows that though the faces of some of them seem quite chaste and charming, yet they notice in their attire licentiousness and pride. I do not say that dignity in the clothing of man or woman is unsuitable but certainly the superfluity or immodest scantiness of clothing is reprehensible.

EXTRAVAGANT DISPLAYS

Also the sin of adornment of apparel is in things that pertain to riding, as in many fine horses that are kept for pleasure that are so fair, fat and expensive and also for many a vicious knave that is kept because of them; and in intricate harnesses, saddles, crops, collars and bridles covered with precious cloth, rich bars and plates of gold and silver. Of this God says by Zechariah the prophet, "I will confound the riders of such horses." These people take little note of the riding of God's son of heaven and of his harness when he rode upon the ass and he had no other harness than the poor clothing of his disciples; nor do we read that he ever rode on any other beast. I say this about the sin of superfluity and not for reasonable honesty when reason requires it.

And certainly, pride is greatly indicated by the holding of a great deal of money when it is of little profit or of no profit; namely when that money is illgotten and damaging to the people because of the insolence of a powerful lord or by way of offices. For certainly, such lords sell their lordships to the devil in hell when they uphold the wickedness of their money. Or else when some folks of low degree, as those who own inns uphold the theft of their inn keepers, and that is done in many deceitful ways. These kinds of people are the flies that follow the honey, or else the hounds that follow the carrion. Such people spiritually strangle their authority, for thus says David the prophet: "Wicked death must come to those rulers and God rules that they must descend down to hell; for in their houses are iniquities and deceitfulness and not the God of heaven." And if they make amends, just as God gave his blessing to Laban by the service of Jacob* and to Pharaoh by the service of Joseph, just so will God give his curse to such rulers who uphold the wickedness of their servants, unless they amend their ways.

Pride of the table appears very often, for certainly, rich men are called to feasts and poor people are sent away and rebuked. Also, when there is an excess of food and drink, namely such kinds of pasties and meat dishes, burning with fire, made pleasing and castellated* with paper and similar wastefulness so that it is a scandal to think of. And also served in too precious vessels and with too much skillful minstrelsy, by which a man is stirred to the pleasures of luxuriousness; if through this he sets his heart less on Jesus Christ, it is a sin, certainly, and in this case, the pleasures might be so great that a man might fall easily by them into mortal sin.

These varied things are the source of Pride, truly, when they are the origin of deliberate evil, considered, premeditated, or else of habit, and are mortal sins, there is no doubt. And when they have their source in undeliberate frailty, and are suddenly refrained from, though they be grievious sins, I guess they are not mortal.

SOURCE OF PRIDE

Now men might ask what is the source of Pride and from what does it spring; I say it sometimes springs from the good in nature and sometimes from the good of fortune and sometimes from the good of grace. Certainly, the good of nature is in either the good of the body or the good of the soul. The goods of the body are health, strength, agility, beauty, gentility and liberty. Goods of the nature of the soul are intelligence, clear understanding, fine skill, natural virtue, good memory. The goods of fortune are wealth, high degrees of lordship, the praises of the people. Goods of grace are wisdom, fortitude, benignity, contemplation, withstanding temptation, and similar things. Of which aforesaid goods, it is certainly folly for a man to pride himself on any of them at all.

Now to speak of the goods of nature, God knows that we sometimes have them as much to our harm as to our profit. To speak of the health of the body, certainly it passes quite quickly, and often it is an indication of the sickness of our soul. For God knows the flesh is a great enemy of the soul, and therefore, the more the body is healthy, the more we are in peril of falling. Thus to pride himself on strength of body is great folly. For the flesh fights against the spirit, and the stronger the flesh is, the sorrier the soul may be. And considering all this, strength of body and worldly well being often cause a man to slip and fall. Also to be proud of his nobility is folly. For often the nobility of the body takes away from the nobility of the soul. We are all of a father and mother, and we are all of a rotten and corrupt nature, both rich and poor. But truly, one type of noble is to be praised, one who adorns a manly heart with virtue and morality which make him a child of Christ. For trust well that whatever man has mastery over sin, that man is a very rough fellow to sin.

Now there are universal signs of nobility such as the eschewing of vice and ribaldry and servitude to sin, in word, in work and in demeanor; and in using virtue, courtesy and purity, and in being liberal, that is being generous, with moderation, for to exceed moderation is folly and sin. Another is to remember the bounty he has received from other people.

Another is to be kind to his good subjects, for as Seneca says, "There is nothing more suitable to a man of high estate than graciousness and compassion. And, therefore, these flies that men call bees, when they choose a king, they choose one that has no stinger

The Virtue of Humility

with which he might sting." Another is for a man to have a noble heart and discipline to achieve very virtuous things. Now certainly, for a man to take pride in the goodness of grace is also an outrageous folly; for this gift of grace that should have turned him to goodness and healing turns him then to corruption and confusion, as Saint Gregory says. Certainly also, whosoever prides himself on good fortune is a very great fool, for sometimes a man is a great lord in the morning and a captive and a wretch by night; and sometimes the wealth of a man is the cause of his death; sometimes the pleasures of a man are the cause of a grievious malady by which he dies. Certainly the praise of the people is sometimes fully false and fickle to trust; today they praise, tomorrow they blame. God knows, the desire to have the approval of the people has caused death to many an anxious man.

HUMILITY
Remedium contra peccatum Superbie.
The Remedy Against the Sin of Pride.

Now since you understand what Pride is and what the kinds of pride are, and whence it springs, now you shall understand what the remedy against the sin of pride is: humility or meekness. That is a virtue through which a man has a full knowledge of himself and considers himself of no worth or value as regards his just deserts, always considering his fraility. Now there are three kinds of humility: humility of the heart; humility of the mouth, and the third is in his works. The humility of the heart is in four ways. One is when a man holds himself worth nothing before God in heaven. Another is when he never despises any other man. Another is when he does not care that men consider him worth nothing. Another is when he is not sad over his humiliation. The humility of mouth is in four things: in modest speech, humble speech, and when he acknowledges with his own mouth that he is just as he thinks he is in his heart. Another is when he praises the goodness of another man and detracts nothing from him. Humility in works is in four ways.

The first is to put other men before himself. The second is to choose the lowest place, overall. The third is to gladly agree to good counsel. The fourth is to gladly stand in the guard of his sovereign, or of him who is of a higher degree. Certainly, that is a great act of humility.

ENVY
Sequitur de Invidia

After Pride, I will speak of the foul sin of Envy, which according to philosophy, is "sadness over other men's prosperity;" and according to the word of Saint Augustine it is "sorrow over other men's well-being and joy over other men's misfortune." This foul sin is plainly against the Holy Ghost. And every sin is against the Holy Ghost for as much as goodness pertains properly to the Holy Ghost and Envy comes properly from evil, therefore, it is properly against the goodness of the Holy Ghost. Now malice is of two kinds: that is to say hardness of heart in wickedness, or else the flesh of man is so blind that he does not consider that he is in sin or does not realize that he is in sin, which is the affliction of the devil.

The other kind of malice is when a man opposes the truth when he knows that it is the truth; and also when he opposes the grace that God has given to his neighbor; all this is through envy. Certainly, then, Envy is the worst sin there is. For truly, other sins are only against one special virtue, but Envy is against all virtues and against all goodness. For it is sorry for all the blessings of his neighbor, and in this way it is different from all other sins. For there is no sin that that has not some delight in itself except for Envy, that always has anguish and sorrow in itself.

The kinds of Envy are these. First there is sorrow at the other man's goodness and prosperity; and prosperity is a natural reason for joy; then Envy is a sin against nature. The second kind of Envy is joy at another man's misfortune, and this is like the devil who always rejoices at man's misfortunes. And from these two sins comes backbiting, and this sin of backbiting or detraction has certain kinds as thus. Some man praises his neighbor with an evil intention,

The Vice of Envy

for he always makes a wicked note at the end. Always he adds a "but" at the end that is indicative of more blame than all the praising is of worth.

The second kind is if a man is good and does or says a thing with a good intention, the backbiter will turn all this goodness upsidedown, for his own shrewd intentions. The third is to make less of the goodness of his neighbor. The fourth kind of back-biting is this. If a man speaks well of a man, then the backbiter will say, "by my faith, yet many a man is better than he;" in detraction of him that men praise. The fifth kind is this: to consent gladly and listen gladly to the evil that men speak of other people. This is a great sin and increases according to the wicked intention of the backbiter.

MURMURING

After backbiting comes complaining or murmur-ing. And sometimes this springs from impatience against God and sometimes against man. It is against God when a man complains about the pains of hell, or about poverty, or about loss of property, or about rain or tempest, or else grouches that wicked people have prosperity or that good men have adversity. All these things man should suffer patiently for they come by the right judgment and ordinance of God. Sometimes complaining comes from avarice as Judas com-plaining against Magdelene when she anointed the head of Our Lord Jesus Christ with her precious oint-ment. This kind of murmuring is such as a man does when he complains about the goodness he himself does or that other people do with their own property. Sometimes the murmuring comes from Pride as when Simon the Pharisee complained against Magdelene when she approached Jesus Christ and wept at his feet for her sins. And sometimes complaining originates in

The Virtue of Charity

Envy; when men reveal a man's faults that were private or accuse him falsely. Complaining is common among servants when their masters tell them to do things they would rather not; and in as much as they dare not openly refuse the orders of their masters, yet they will say evil and complain and grouch privately for spite; such words men call the devil's *Pater Noster* though the devil never had *a Pater Noster,* yet lewd folk give it such a name. Sometimes it comes from anger or secret hatred that nourishes rancor in the heart as I shall explain later. Then bitterness of heart comes through which every good deed of his neighbor seems to him bitter and unsavory. Then comes discord that breaks all kinds of friendships. Then comes contempt for his neighbor, whatever he does. Then comes accusation when a man seeks occasion to annoy his neighbor, which is like the craft of the devil who waits day and night to accuse us all.

Then comes malice through which a man annoys his neighbor privately, if he can, and if he cannot, he will find some way to work his wicked will, as in burning down his house secretly, or poisoning or slaying his animals, and similar things.

CHARITY
Remedium contra peccatum Invidie
The Remedy against the Sin of Envy

Now I will speak of remedies against this foul sin of envy. First is loving God above all things and loving his neighbor as himself; for truly one may not be without the other. And trust well that in the name of your neighbor, you shall understand the name *brother,* for we all have one earthly father and one mother, that is to say Adam and Eve, and also one spiritual father and that is the God of heaven. You are accountable to love your neighbor and wish him all good things.

Therefore, says God, "Love thy neighbor as thyself," that is to say to the salvation of both life and soul. Moreover, you shall love him in word, and in kindly chastising and admonnishing, and comfort him in his troubles, and pray for him with all your heart. And you shall love him in deeds in such a way that you shall do to him in charity as you would that it were done to you in your own person. And, therefore, you shall not do him any harm through wicked word, nor harm to his body, nor to his property, nor to his soul by the temptation of evil example. You shall not desire his wife nor any of his things. Understand also that in the word *neighbor* is understood *enemy*. Certainly man should love his enemy, by the commandment of God, and truly, your friend shall you also love in God. I say your enemy you shall love for God's sake, by his commandment. For if it were right that man should hate his enemy, truly God would not receive us who have been his enemies into his love. He shall do three things as follows against three kinds of wrong his enemy could do to him. Against hatred and rancor of heart, he shall love him in his heart. Against scolding or wicked words, he shall pray for his enemy. Against the wicked deeds of his enemy, he shall do him good for Christ says: "Love your enemies and pray for those who speak evil against you; and also for those you chase and pursue, and do good to those you hate." Thus Our Lord Jesus Christ commands us to do to our enemies. For truly, nature drives us to love our friends, and by my faith, our enemies have more need of love than our friends; and to them that have more need, certainly to them should men do good; and in this deed we have remembrance of Jesus Christ who died for his enemies. And in as much as this same love is more difficult for us to perform, so much greater is the merit; and, therefore, the loving of our enemy has confounded the venom of the devil. For just as the devil is confounded by humility, so he is wounded to the death by our love of our enemy. Certainly, then, love is the medicine that casts the venom of envy out of man's heart. The steps of this shall be more fully explained in the following chapter.

The Vice of Anger

ANGER
Sequitur de Ira

After Envy I will describe the sin of Anger for surely, whoever has envy of his neighbor will commonly be found to have Anger by word or deed against him whom he envies. And Anger comes from Pride as well as Envy, for he who is proud or envious is easily irritated.

This sin of Anger, according to the explanation of Saint Augustine, is a wicked wish to be avenged by word or deed. Anger, according to the Philosopher, is the hot blood of a man kindled in his heart through which he would do harm to him that he hates. For certainly the heart of a man by the burning and racing of his blood grows so troubled that he is without good judgment or reason. But you should understand that anger is in two forms: one of them is good; the other, evil. The good anger is through jealousy of goodness wherein a man is angry with wickedness and at wickedness. And, therefore, a wise man says that anger is better than jest. This anger is with calmness and it is anger without bitterness; not angry against the man but against the misdeeds of the man as the prophet David says, *"Irascimini et nolite peccare" (Be angry but sin not)*. Now understand that evil anger is of two kinds; that is to say sudden or hasty anger without the advice and consent of reason. The meaning and sense of this is that the reason of the man has not consented to this sudden anger and in that case it is venial.

VENGEANCE

Another anger is much more wicked that comes from meanness of heart, realized and considered, with an evil desire to do vengeance, and, therefore, his reason consents. And truly this is a mortal sin. This

Anger is so displeasing to God that it troubles the planets and chases the Holy Ghost out of a man's soul, and wastes and destroys the likeness of God, that is to say the virtue that is in man's soul, and puts him in the likeness of the devil and separates him from God that is his rightful Lord. This Anger is a very great delight to the devil for it is the devil's furnace that is enkindled with the fire of hell. For just as fire is more powerful to destroy all earthly things than any other element, Anger is more powerful to destroy all spiritual things. Look how the fire of small live coals that have been almost dead under the ashes quicken again when they are touched with brimstone; just so Anger will always quicken again when touched with the Pride that is hidden in man's heart. For certainly, fire does not come out of nothing unless it were first in something naturally, as fire is drawn out of flint with steel. And just as pride is often times the material of Anger, just so rancor nourishes and preserves Anger. There is a kind of tree, says Saint Isadore, that when men make fire from that tree and cover the coals of it with ashes, truly, the fire will last a year or more. And that is the way it is with rancor, when it is once conceived in the heart of some men, it will last from one Easter Day to the next Easter Day and longer. Certainly such a man is far from the mercy of God all that while.

In the aforesaid devil's furnace are forged three curses: Pride that always blows and increases the fire by chiding and wicked words; then Envy stands and holds the hot iron on the heart of man with a pair of long tongs of rancor; and then stands the sin of Contumely or strife and quarrels and battles and forges by rude reproaches. Certainly this cursed sin annoys both the man himself and also his neighbor. For truly, almost all the harm that a man does to his neighbor comes from wrath. For surely outrageous wrath does all the devil commands him; he spares neither Christ nor his sweet Mother. And in his outrageous anger and wrath, alas! alas! many a one feels in his heart full wickedly toward both Christ and all his saints. Is this not a cursed vice ? Yes, certainly. Alas! It separates a man from his wit and reason and all his happy spiritual life that should preserve his soul. Certainly, it takes away God's dominion, and that is man's soul and the love of his neighbor. It strives also all day against truth. It robs him of the quiet of his heart and subverts his soul.

MURDER

From Anger come these stinking progeny: first hatred that is old wrath; discord, through which a man forsakes his old friend that he has loved a long time; and then comes war and every kind of wrong that man does to his neighbor, in body or in property. From this cursed sin of Anger also comes murder. And understand that homicide, that is murder, is in various ways. Some kinds of murder are spiritual and some are bodily. Spiritual manslaughter is in six things. First in hate, as says Saint John, "he that hates his brother is a murderer." Homicide is also by backbiting of whom Solomon says that "they have two swords with which they slay their neighbors." For surely, it is as wicked to take away their good name as their life. Homicide is also in giving evil counsel by fraud; as to give counsel to raise accounts and payments. Of that Solomon says: "Roaring lions and hungry bears are like cruel lords who withhold or cut the reward or payment or the wages of servants, or else charge interest, or steal from the alms of the poor." For this the wise man says, "Feed him who almost dies of hunger," truly, unless if you feed him, you slay him; and all these are deadly sins.

MANSLAUGHTER

Bodily manslaughter is when you slay him with your tongue, as when you command one to kill a man or you give him counsel to kill a man. Manslaughter in deed is in four ways. One is by law as when a judge condemns a man who is guilty to death. But let the judge beware that he act rightly and not for the desire to spill blood but for the keeping of justice. Another homicide is what is done out of necessity as when a man kills another in self-defense and may not otherwise escape from his own death. But if he may escape without killing his adversary, and still kills him, it is a sin and he shall do penance as for a deadly sin. Also if a man by chance or adventure, shot an arrow or cast a stone with which he killed a man, it is homicide. Also if a woman, by negligence, rolls on top of her child in her sleep, it is homicide and a deadly sin.

CONTRACEPTION AND ABORTION

Also when a man interrupts the conception of a child and makes a woman either barren by drinking harmful herbs so that she may not conceive, or slays a child by drinking willfully, or else puts certain things in her secret places to kill the child, or else does unnatural sin by which man or woman diffuses their nature in a way or a place so that a child may not be conceived, or else a woman having conceived, hurts herself and kills the child, that is homicide. What say we of women that murder their children for fear of worldly shame ? Certainly a horrible homicide. It is also homicide if a man approaches a woman through the desire of lechery, through which the child perishes, or else hits a woman knowingly through which she loses her child. All these are homicides and horrible deadly sins.

Yet from Anger come many more sins in word, in thought and in deed; for example, he who imputes to God or blames God for things of which he himself is guilty, or despises God and all his saints as do these cursed gamblers in several countries. This cursed sin they commit when they feel in their heart hateful toward God and all his saints. Also when they treat irreverently the sacrament of the altar; this sin is so great that it can scarce be forgiven, except that the mercy of God passes all his works; it is so great, he is so kind.

Then a poisonous anger comes from Ire. When a man is sharply admonished in confession to stop his sin, then he will answer hotly and angrily, and defend or excuse by the frailty of the flesh, or else he did it for fellowship with his friends or he says the devil tempted him, or he did it because of his youth, or his disposition is so brave that he may not forbear, or it is his destiny, as he says, until a certain age, or else he says it is due to the nobility of his ancestors, and this kind of thing. All these people wrap themselves in their sins so that they do not free themselves. For truly, no creature that excuses himself willfully may be delivered from his sin till he meekly acknowledges his sin.

SWEARING

After these sins, then, comes swearing, which is expressly against the commandment of God; and this is done often out of wrath or anger. God says: "You shall not take the name of the Lord thy God in vain or in idleness." Also, Our Lord Jesus Christ says by the word of Saint Matthew, "You shall not swear in any manner; neither by heaven for it is God's throne; nor by earth for it is his footstool; nor by Jerusalem for it is the city of a great king; nor by your head for you may not make a hair of it white or black. Say by your word 'yes, yes,' and 'no, no,' and more than that is of evil." Thus says Christ. For Christ's sake do not swear sinfully in the dismembering of Christ by soul, heart, bones and body. For certainly it seems that you think that the cursed Jews did not dismember the precious person of Christ enough but you must dismember him more. And if it be that the law compels you to swear, then follow the law of God in your swearing, as Jeremiah says, *quarto capitulo:* " You shall keep three conditions: you shall swear in truth, in judgement and in justice." That is to say you shall swear truthfully, for every lie is against Christ. For Christ is Truth itself.

And consider this, every great swearer, not compelled by law to swear, the plague shall not depart from his house while he uses such illicit swearing. You shall swear in judgment when you are constrained by your judge to witness to the truth. Also you shall not swear out of envy, nor for favors, nor for bribes but for justice, for declaration of it, to the honor of God and the help of your fellow Christians. And, therefore, every man who takes God's name in vain, or swears falsely with his mouth, or takes on himself the name of Christ in being called a Christian, and lives not by Christ's teaching and life, they take God's name in vain. Consider what Saint Peter says, "There is no other name under heaven given to men by which they may be saved;" that is to say but the name of Jesus Christ.

Take note also how precious the name of Christ is, as Saint Paul says " that in the name of Jesus every knee of heavenly creatures, or earthly, or in hell shall bow." For it is so great and so worthy of worship that the cursed fiend in hell should tremble to hear it named. Then it seems that men who swear so horribly by his blessed name despise it more boldly than did the cursed Jews, or else the devil that trembles when he hears that name. Now certainly, since swearing, unless it be lawfully done, is forbidden, much worse is foreswearing falsely and needlessly.

What have we to say of him who delights in swearing and considers it noble or manly to swear great oaths ? And what of them that in common usage never cease swearing great oaths, although the cause is not worth a straw ? Certainly, this is a horrible sin. Swearing suddenly without deliberation is also a sin.

Let us go now to the horrible sins of conjuring as is done by false enchanters or necromancers in basins full of water, or in a bright sword, in a circle, in a fire, or in a shoulder bone of a sheep. I must say they act cursedly and damnably against Christ and all the faith of holy church.

What say we of those who believe in omens as by the flight or the noise of birds or of animals or by lot or by divination or of figures drawn on the ground, by dreams, by creakings of doors, by cracking of houses, by gnawing of rats, and such wretched things ? Certainly all these things are forbidden by God and his holy church. They who set their beliefs on such filth are cursed until they amend their ways. Charms for wounds or diseases of men or animals, if they take any effect, it may be because God allows it for people should give more faith and reverence to his name.

LYING

Now I will speak of lying which generally is giving a false meaning to a word with the intention of deceiving his fellow Christian. There is some lying which gives no advantage to any creature, and some lying turns to the ease and profit of one man and to the harm and damage of another man. Another form of lying is to save one's life or one's property. Another form of lying comes from the pleasure of lying, in which delight they will forge a long tale and paint it with all circumstances wherein all the ground of the tale is false. Some lying comes because a man wishes to uphold his word, and some lying comes from uncounseled recklessness, and similar things.

Now let us touch on the vice of flattery which is not given gladly but out of fear or out of greed. Generally, flattery is wrongful praise. Flatterers are the devil's novices that nourish his children with the milk of flattery. For truly, Solomon says that "flattery is worse than detraction," for sometimes detraction will make a proud man humble, for he dreads criticism, but certainly it is flattery that makes a man conceited in his heart and demeanor. Flatterers are the devil's enchanters for they make a man think that he is what he is not. They are like Judas who betray a man to sell him to his enemy, that is, to the devil. Flatterers are the devil's chaplains that ever sing *Placebo*. Place flattery in the vices of Anger, for often times if one man is angry with another, then he will flatter some creature to uphold him in his quarrel.

CURSING

We will speak now of such cursing as comes from an angry heart. Cursing may be seen a power house of harm. Such cursing separates man from the reign of God, as Saint Paul says. And oftentimes, the cursing returns to him who cursed, as a bird returns again to his own nest. Above all, men ought not to curse their children, and give to the devil his progeny, as far as is in him. Certainly it is a great danger and a great sin.

SCOLDING AND SCORNING

Let us speak now of scolding and reproach which cause great wounds in a man's heart for they unsew the seams of friendship in man's heart. For certainly, it is difficult for a man to be at peace with him who has reviled him openly and reproved him and reproached him. This is a grisly sin, as Christ said in the gospel. And consider now that he that reproves his neighbor, he shames him either for some injury or pain of his body such as leprosy or "croked harlot" or for some sin that he has done. Now if he shames him for some bodily harm, then the shame turns to Jesus Christ for pain is by the wise visitation of God and by his sufferance, be it leprosy, injury or disease. And if he reprove him of sin in an uncharitable manner such as "you adulterer" or "you drunken harlot", then that causes the devil to rejoice who ever is happy when men commit sin. And certainly, chiding may not come from anything but a villainous heart. For out of the fullness of the heart the mouth speaks, very often.

And you should understand when you see any man scolding another that he should beware of scolding and reproving. For truly, unless he is careful he may quicken the fire of anger and wrath which he should quench and perhaps slay him whom he might have chastised more kindly. For as Solomon says, "The amiable tongue is the tree of life," that is to say the spiritual life; and truly an immoderate tongue slays the spirit of him that scolds and also him that is scolded. Consider what Saint Augustine says: "There is nothing so like the devil's child as he who often chides."

Saint Paul, also, says, "A servant of God profits not to chide." And that chiding is a villainous thing between all kinds of people, yet it is certainly most common between a man and his wife; for there is never rest. And therefore, Solomon says, "A house that is leaking and in disarray and a scolding wife are alike." A man that is in a house that leaks in many places, although he avoids the dripping in one place, it falls on him in another. So it is with a scolding wife;

she chides him in one place or she chides him in another. And therefore, "better a morsel of bread with joy than a house full of delicacies with scolding," says Solomon. Saint Paul says, "O women, be subject to your husbands, as it behooves you in God; husbands, love your wives."

Next we will speak of scorning which is a wicked sin, namely when one scorns a man for his good works. For certainly, such scorners are like the foul toad who cannot bear to smell the sweet odor of the vine when it flourishes. These scorners are fellows who party with the devil; for they have joy when the devil wins and sorrow when he loses. They are adversaries of Jesus Christ for they hate what he loves, that is to say the salvation of the soul.

BAD COUNSEL

Next we will speak of wicked counsel for he that gives evil counsel is a traitor for he deceives him that trusts in him, as *Achitofel et Absolonem*. But nevertheless, his wicked counsel is first against himself. For as the wise man says, "Every false lie has this in it, that he that would hurt another man hurts first himself." And men should understand they should not take the counsel of false folk nor angry folk nor vexed folk, nor people who love their own profit too much, nor people too worldly, namely in the counselling of souls.

Now comes the sin of those who sow discord between people and that Christ really hates. And no wonder, for he died to make peace. And they do more shame to Christ than those who crucified him, for God loves friendship among people better than he did his own body which he gave for unity. Therefore, they are like the devil who are ever about making discord.

Now comes the sin of double tongued people who speak nicely in front of people and wickedly behind their backs; or else they pretend they speak with a good intention, or else in fun or jest, and yet they speak with evil intention. Now comes the betrayal of confidences by which a man is dishonored, certainly unless the doer may repair the damage.

Now comes threats, an obvious folly; for he that often threatens, threatens more than he can perform most of the time.

IDLE WORDS

Now come idle words that are without profit to those that speak the words or to those that listen to them. Or else idle words are those that are unnecessary or without intention of any normal profit. And idle words are sometimes venial sins and men should beware of them for we shall give a reckoning of them before God.

Now comes chattering, that may not be without sin. As Solomon says, "It is an obvious sign of foolishness." A philosopher said when men asked him how a man should please the people, he answered, "Do many good works and speak few idle words."

After this comes the sin of jesters that have been the devil's apes, for they make people laugh at their jokes as people do at the pranks of an ape. Saint Paul condemned such jokes. Look how virtuous and holy words comfort those that labor in the service of Christ; just so the villainous words and monkeyshines of jesters comfort those that work in the service of the devil. These are the sins of the tongue that come from anger and other sins.

The Virtue of Patience

MEEKNESS AND PATIENCE
Sequitur remedium contra peccatum Ire
REMEDIES AGAINST THE SIN OF ANGER

The remedy against Anger is the virtue that men call meekness, that is graciousness, and also another virtue that men call patience or sufferance. Graciousness controls and restrains the stirring of man's feelings in the heart in such a way that they do not skip out in anger or wrath. Sufferance suffers sweetly all the annoyances and wrongs that men do to man openly. Saint Jerome says this of gentleness, that "it neither does nor says anything injurious to any creature for no injury that men do or say inflames his reason." This virtue sometimes comes naturally, but, as the philosopher says, "man is an intelligent thing, by nature gracious and inclined to goodness, but when good nature is informed with grace, then it is worth more."

Patience is another remedy against Anger; it is a virtue that suffers sweetly every man's goodness and is not angry at injury that is done to him. The philosopher says that patience is the virtue that suffers graciously all the outrages of adversity and every wicked word. This virtue makes a man like God and makes him God's own dear child, as Christ says. This virtue discomforts your enemy. And therefore, the wise man says, "If you would vanquish your enemy, learn to be patient." And you should understand man suffers four kinds of grievances in outward things, against which he should have four kinds of patience.

The first grievance is wicked words. This same Jesus Christ suffered very patiently without complaining when the Jews despised and reproached him often. Suffer then patiently, for the wise man says, "If you strive with a fool, if the fool be angry or if he laugh, either way you shall have no rest." The other outward grievance is to have damage to your property. There again Christ suffered very patiently when he was despoiled of all he had in this life and that was nothing but his clothes. and the third grievance is for a man to have bodily harm. That Christ suffered patiently in all his passion. The fourth grievance is in outrageous labor in work. Therefore, I say that people who make their servants work excessively hard or at an unsuitable time, as on holy days, truly do a great sin. Here again Christ suffered patiently and taught us patience when he bore upon his blessed shoulders the cross upon which he would suffer a shameful death. Here men may learn to be patient, for certainly not only are Christians patient for the love of Jesus Christ and for the reward of the blissful life that is eternal, but certainly the old pagans that never were Christian admired and used the virtue of patience.

Once upon a time a philosopher that would have beaten his pupil for his trespasses which had upset him greatly brought a stick to scourge the child, and when the child saw the stick, he said to his master, "What do you think you do ?" "I will beat you," said the master, "for your correction." "Forsooth," said the child, "you ought first to correct yourself who has lost all patience for the guilt of a child." "Forsooth," said the master weeping, "You speak the truth. Take the stick, my dear son, and correct me for my impatience."

From patience comes obedience through which a man is obedient to Christ and to all those to whom he ought to be obedient in Christ. And understand that obedience is perfect when a man does all he should do gladly and quickly and with a good heart. Obedience is to fulfill the doctrine of God and of his sovereigns to which he ought to be obedient in all justice.

SLOTH
Sequitur de Accidia

After the sins of Envy and of Anger I will speak of Sloth. Envy blinds the heart of a man and Anger troubles a man and Sloth makes him sad, anxious, and fretful. Envy and Ire make bitterness in the heart which bitterness is the mother of Sloth and separates him from the love of all goodness. Then Sloth is the anguish of a troubled heart. Saint Augustine says, "It is the vexation of goodness and the joy of evil." Certainly this is a damnable sin, for it does wrong to Jesus Christ in as much as it prevents the service that men ought to do to Christ with all diligence as Solomon says. But Sloth does no such diligence. He does all things with annoyance and with fretfulness, with slackness and excuses, with idleness and disinclination; for which the book says, "Cursed be he that does the service of God negligently."

Then Sloth is the enemy to every state of man, for the estate of man is in three manners. First is the estate of innocence as was the state of Adam before he fell into sin; in that state his occupation was to worship and praise and adore God. Another estate is that of sinful man in which he must labor in praying to God for the foregiveness of his sins and that God will grant him to arise out of his sinfulness. Another state is the state of grace in which estate he continues works of penance. And certainly to all these things Sloth is an enemy and contrary, for Sloth loves no industriousness at all. Now this foul sin of Sloth is an enemy to the livelihood of the body for it has no providence against temporal necessities, for it wastes and spoils all good temporalities by recklessness.

The fourth thing is that Sloth is like those that are in the pains of hell because of their laziness and their sadness, for those that have been damned are so bound

The Vice of Sloth

that they cannot do well nor think well. Because of Sloth a man is annoyed and encumbered so that he cannot do any good works; God abominates such sloth, as Saint John says.

Now comes Sloth that will not bear anything difficult nor any penance. For truly, Sloth is so tender and so delicate, as Solomon says, that he will not bear any difficulties nor penances and, therefore, he ruins all that he does. Against this rotten-hearted sin of Sloth, man should exert himself to do good works and take the courage, manly and virtuously, to do them well. Remember Our Lord Jesus Christ notes every good deed, be it ever so little. Labor is a great thing, for it makes the laborer, as Saint Bernard says, have strong arms and hard muscles, and Sloth makes him feeble and soft. Then comes a fear to begin any good works. For certainly, he that is inclined to sin thinks it is too great an effort to undertake works of goodness, and in his heart decides that good works are so difficult and so burdensome that he dare not undertake them, as Saint Gregory says.

DESPAIR

Now comes despair, that is despair of the mercy of God that comes sometimes from too much sorrow and sometimes from too much fear, imagining that he has done so much sin that nothing will avail him even if he repented and forsook his sin; through this despair, he abandons his heart to every kind of sin, says Saint Augustine. This damnng sin, if it is continued to its end is called the sin against the Holy Ghost. This horrible sin is so dangerous that he that is in despair does not fear to do any felony or sin, as shown well by Judas. Certainly, then, this sin above all sins is most displeasing to Christ and most hostile.

Truly, he that despairs is like the cowardly knight that shouts, "I give up" without need. Alas! Alas! needless is he cowardly and needlessly despairing. Certainly the mercy of God is ever ready to the penitent and above all his works. Alas! can a man not recall the gospel of *Saint Luke*, 15, where Christ says, "as well shall there be joy in heaven upon a sinful man that does penance as upon ninety-nine just men that need no penance." Look further in the same gospel to the joy and feasting of the good man who had lost his son, when the repentent son was returned to his father. Can they not also remember that as *Saint Luke* says, 23, how the thief that was hanged beside Jesus Christ said, "Lord remember me when you come into your kingdom ?" "For truly," said Christ, "I say to you, today you shall be with me in Paradise." Certainly there is no sin of man so horrible that it may not, in his life, be destroyed by penance, through the virtue of the passion and death of Christ. Alas! Why does man need to despair when the mercy of Christ is so ready and so great ? Ask and receive.

SOMNOLENCE

Then comes somnolence, that is sluggish slumbering which makes a man heavy and dull in body and soul; this sin comes from Sloth. And certainly, by way of reason, the time that men should not sleep is the morning, unless there were reasonable cause. For the morning is the most suitable time for a man to say his prayers and to think of God and to honor God and to give alms to the poor that come first in the name of Christ. Look what Solomon says, " Whosoever would waken in the morning and seek me, he shall find me." Then comes negligence or recklessness that takes heed of nothing. And as ignorance is the mother of all harm, negligence is the nursemaid. Negligence does not care when he does a thing whether he does it well or badly.

Of the remedy of these two sins, the wise man says, "He that fears God does not spare himself in doing what he ought to do." And he that loves God will work diligently to please God and strive with all his might to do well.

Then comes idleness that is the gate of all evil. An idle man is like a place that has no walls. The devil may enter on every side or shoot temptations at him who is unprotected, from every side. This idleness is the sink of all wicked and villainous thoughts, of all gossip, trifling, and all filth. Certainly heaven is given to him who will labor and not to idle people. And David says, "they that have not been among the laborers shall not be whipped with them;" that is to say, in purgatory. Certainly it seems then that they shall be tormented with the devil in hell, unless they do penance.

TARDINESS

Then comes the sin that men call *tarditas,* as when man is slow or tardy in turning to God. That certainly is great folly. He is like the man who falls in the ditch and will not get out. This vice comes from the false hope that he shall live long but that hope often fails.

Then comes indolence; that is he that, when he begins any good work, leaves it and stops, as do they who have any creature to govern take no care of them if they find it difficult or annoying. These are the new shepherds that knowingly let their sheep run to the wolf that is in the bushes, or do not take care of their own domain. From this comes poverty and destruction both in spiritual and temporal things. Then comes a cold manner that freezes the heart of man. Then comes lack of devotion through which a man is blinded, as Saint Bernard says, and has such languor of soul that he may neither read nor sing in holy church, nor hear nor think of any devotion, nor work with his hands at good works, for they are unappealing and disagreeable to him. Then he grows slothful and lazy and soon he will be angry, and soon inclined to hate and envy. Then comes the sin of worldly sorrow called *tristicia,* that kills a man, as Saint Paul says. For certainly such sorrow works to the death of the soul and the body also; for from that a man is annoyed with his own life. Often such sorrow shortens the life of a man before his time comes by natural causes.

FORTITUDE
Remedium contra peccatum Accidie
REMEDY AGAINST THE SIN OF SLOTH

Against this horrible sin of Sloth and its branches, there is a virtue called *fortitudo* or strength. That is an affection by which man scorns troublesome things. This virtue is so mighty and so vigorous that is dares to fight mightily and wisely keeps himself from wicked dangers, and wrestles against the assaults of the devil. For it strengthens and gives force to the soul, just as Sloth weakens it and makes it feeble. Through *fortitudo,* a man may endure suitable work by long-suffering.

The virtue has many kinds; the first is called magnanimity, that is to say great courage. For certainly it takes great courage against Sloth, lest it swell the soul with the sin of sorrow or destroy it by despair. This virtue makes people undertake difficult things by their own will, wisely and reasonably. And in as much as the devil fights man more by slyness and trickery than by strength, men should fight him by reason, by intelligence, and by discretion. Then there are the virtues of faith and hope in God and his Saints

The Virtue of Fortitude

to achieve and accomplish the good works in which he firmly purposes to continue. Then comes security or confidence; that is when a man does not get discouraged with the good works he has begun. Then comes magnificence, that is to say when a man performs great works of goodness; and that is why men should do good works for in the accomplishing of great good works lies the great reward. Then there is constancy, that is stability of courage; and this should be in the heart by steadfast faith, and in the mouth and in the bearing and in the affections and in deeds. Also there are special remedies against Sloth in various works, and in the consideration of the pains of hell and of the joys of heaven, and in the trust in the grace of the Holy Ghost, that will give a man strength to fulfill his good intentions.

Avarice follows.
Sequitur de Avaricia .

AVARICE
Sequitur de Avaricia

After Sloth I will speak of Avarice and of Covetousness, of which Saint Paul says, "The root of all evil is covetousness." For truly, when the heart of man is confounded in itself and troubled and the soul has lost the comfort of God, then he seeks an idle solace in worldly things.

Avarice, according to the description of Saint Augustine, is a heartfelt desire to have earthly things. Some other people say that Avarice is purchasing many earthly things and giving nothing to those that are in need. And understand, Avarice is not only in regard to land or property but sometimes in knowledge or glory and every kind of outrageous thing is Avarice and Covetousness. The difference between Avarice and Covetousness is this. Covetousness is to desire such things as you do not have, and Avarice is to withhold and keep such things as you have, without a just need. Truly this Avarice is a sin that is damnable for all holy scripture curses it and speaks against that vice for it does wrong to Jesus Christ. For it takes from him the love men owe to him and turns it backwards, against all reason, and makes the avaricious man have more hope in his property than in Jesus Christ and pays more attention to the keeping of his treasure than he does to the service of Jesus Christ. And therefore Saint Paul says that an avaricious man is the slave of idolatry.

What difference is there between and idolater and an avaricious man except that the idolater has, perhaps, an idol or two and the avaricious man has many ? For certainly, every florin in his coffer is his idol. And certainly the sin of idolatry is the first thing God forbade in the ten commandments, as is witnessed in *Exodus 20:* "Thou shalt have no false Gods before

The Vice of Avarice

me, nor shall you make to yourself an graven image."
Thus an avaricious man who loves his treasure before
God is an idolater through this cursed sin of avarice.
From covetousness come difficult affairs where men
are obsessed with business dealings, customs, and
taxes, more than duty or reason demands. And also
they take from their bondsmen exactions or fines,
which might be more rightly called extortions than
exactions. Of these exactions and ransomings of
bondsmen, some lord's stewards say that it is just in
as much as a churl has no temporal thing that is not his
lord's, as they say. But certainly these lords do wrong
to take from their bondsfolk things they never gave
them. Saint Augustine says that truly that is the con-
dition of slavery and the first reason for slavery is sin.

Thus you may see that the guilty deserve servi-
tude but not by nature, not by way of being born.
Therefore, these lords should not glory in their posi-
tion since by natural conditions they are not lords over
thralls but that slavery comes as the reward for sin.
And furthermore, as the law says that temporal goods
of bondsmen are the goods of the lord, that is to be
understood, the goods of the emperor to defend him in
justice, but not to be robbed of them or plundered.
And, therefore, Seneca says, "Thy prudence should
live benignly with your slaves." These that you call
your slaves are God's people; humble folk are Christ's
friends; they are intimate with the Lord.

Remember also that from the same seed that
churls spring, lords also spring. The churl may be
saved as well as the lord. The same death that takes the
churl shall also take the lord. Concerning this I read,
do justly with your churl as you would your lord did
with you, if you were in his place. Every sinful man
is a churl to sin. I advise you, lords, to work in such a
way with your churls, that they love you rather than
fear you. I know well that there are degrees above

degrees, as is reasonable, and there is argument that men do their duty as they should, but certainly, extortions and contempt of your underlings is damnable.

And understand, furthermore, that conquerors and tyrants very often make slaves of of those born with as royal blood as they themselves. This name of slavery was never known until Noah said that his son Caan should be a slave to his brother because of sin. What do you say then of those who rob and do extortions to holy church ? Certainly the sword that men first give to a knight when he is dubbed signifies that he should defend holy church and not rob or pillage it; and whosoever does that is a traitor to Christ. As Saint Augustine says, "They are the devil's wolves that strangle the sheep of Jesus Christ," and do worse than wolves. For truly, when the wolf has filled his stomach, he stops strangling the sheep. But truly, the plunderers and destroyers of God's holy church do not do so for they never stop stealing. Now as I have said, since sin was the first cause of slavery, then it is thus that the same time all the world was in sin, then all this world was in slavery and subjection. But certainly, since the time of grace came, God ordained that some people should be higher in station and degree, and some people lower, that everyone should be served in his state and degree. And, therefore, in some countries where they have slaves, when they have turned the slave to the faith, they make them free from their slavery. And, therefore, the lord has obligations to his man and the man has obligations to his lord. The Pope calls himself the servant of the servants of God; but the state of holy church might not have been, the general welfare might not have been, nor peace and rest in the earth except that God ordained that some men had a higher degree and some men a lower, therefore sovereignty was ordained to keep and maintain and defend their underlings or their reasonable subjects as it is within their power and not to destroy nor confound them.

Therefore, I say that these same lords are like wolves that wrongfully devour the possessions or the property of poor folk, without mercy or measure. They should receive the mercy of Jesus Christ by the same measure that they have measured to poor folk, unless they amend. Now comes deceit between merchant and merchant. And you shall understand that there are many kinds of merchandise; one is bodily and the other is spiritual; one is honest and lawful, the other is dishonest and unlawful. Of bodily merchandise what is lawful and honest is this: if, as God has ordained, a ruler or country is sufficient unto itself, then it is lawful that out of the abundance of this country, men help another country that is more needy. And, therefore, there must be merchants to bring the goods of the one country to the other. Other trading that men are accustomed to carry on by fraud, treachery, deceit, lying, and false oaths is cursed and damnable.

SIMONY

Spiritual merchandise is principally simony, that is an intense desire to buy spiritual things, that is things that pertain to the sanctuary of God and the supervision of the soul. This desire, if a man try diligently to fulfill it, albeit to no effect, is still a deadly sin to him, and if he be of a religious order, he is in violation of his rule. Simony is named for Simon Magus who would have bought with temporal property the gift that God had given by the Holy Ghost to Saint Peter and to the apostles. And, therefore, understand that both he that buys and he that sells spiritual things are called simoniacs, be it by property, be it by procuring, by carnal begging of his friends, lay friends, or spiritual friends. Carnal ("fleshly") is of two kinds;

by kindred or by other friends. Truly, if they plead for him that is not worthy and able, it is simony, if he takes the benefice and if he is worthy and able, there is none. The other manner is when men or women beg for the advancement of another person out of the wicked, carnal affection that they have for the person, and that is foul simony. But certainly, in service, for which men give spiritual things to their servants, it must be understood that the service must be honest, and also without bargaining, and the person must be qualified. As Saint Damasus says, " All the sins of the world are as nothing compared to this sin." For it is the greatest sin that could be after the sin of Lucifer and the Antichrist. For by this sin, God loses the church and the soul he bought with his precious blood, by those that give churches to those who are not worthy. For they put in thieves that steal the souls belonging to Jesus Christ and destroy his patrimony. Because of such priests and curates, low men have less   reverence for the sacraments of holy church; and such givers of churches put out the children of Christ, and put into the church the devil's own son. They sell the souls of the lambs they should take care of to the wolf that strangles them. And, therefore, they shall never have a part in the pasture of the lambs, that is in the bliss of heaven.

GAMBLING.

And now comes gambling with the accompanying tables of backgammon and raffles, from which come deceits. false oaths, scoldings, ravings, blaspheming, renouncing God, hatred of neighbors, wasting of his goods, wasting his time, and sometimes murder. Certainly, gamblers are not without great sin while they pursue that craft. From Avarice, also, come lying, theft, false witness, and false oaths. And you should understand that these are great sins and expressly against the commandments of God, as I have said.

FALSE WITNESS

False witness is in word and also in deed. In word it is to take away your neighbors good name by witnessing falsely or taking away his property or his inheritance by your false witnessing, when out of anger, or for reward, or out of envy, you bear false witness or accuse him, or excuse him by your false witness, or else excuse yourself falsely. Beware of jurors and scribes! Certainly Suzanna was in great sorrow and pain because of false witnessing, and so were many others.

THEFT

The sin of theft is also expressly against God's command, and it is of two manners, corporal and spiritual. Corporal is to take your neighbors property against his will whether by force or by trickery, by mete or by measure, by stealing or by false indictments upon him, or by borrowing your neighbor's property, never intending to repay it, and similar things.

SACRILEGE

Spiritual theft is sacrilege, that is to say, harming holy things or things sacred to Christ. That is in two ways: by reason of the holy place such as churches or church yards, for which every wicked thing that man does in such places may be called sacrilege, or every act of violence in the same places; also, they that falsely withhold the rights that belong to holy church. And plainly and generally, sacrilege is to rob holy things from holy places, or unholy things from holy places or holy things from unholy places.

GENEROSITY, MERCY, PITY
Remedium contra peccatum Avaricie
REMEDIES AGAINST THE SIN OF AVARICE

Now you should understand that the cure for Avarice is mercy and pity in large measure. And men might ask why mercy and pity cure Avarice. Certainly the avaricious man shows no mercy nor pity for the needy man for he delights in keeping his treasure and not in rescuing or relieving his fellow Christian. And, therefore, I speak first of mercy. Mercy, as the philosopher says, is a virtue by which a man's heart is moved by the misery of him who is in trouble. This feeling of mercy is followed by pity in performing the charitable works of mercy. And certainly these things move a man to pity for Jesus Christ who gave himself for our sins, and suffered death for mercy, and forgave us our original sins, and thereby released us from the pains of hell, and lessened the pains of purgatory by penance, and gives us the grace to do well and at last reach the bliss of heaven. The kinds of mercy are to loan and to give, to forgive and remit, to have pity in the heart and compassion on the misery of his fellow Christian, and also to chastise when there is need.

Another kind of remedy against Avarice is reasonable largesse or generosity; but truly, here it is well to consider the grace of Jesus Christ, and of the temporal goods and also eternal goods that Christ gave to us; and to remember the death we shall receive, we know not when nor how, and also that we shall leave all that we have except what we have spent in good works.

But, in as much as some people are intemperate, men should avoid foolish largesse that men call waste. Certainly he that is foolish does not give his property but loses his property. Certainly, what he gives for

The Virtue of Generosity

personal glory to minstrels and to folk to make himself well known in the world, he has sinned by this and not given alms. Certainly he wastes his goods who seeks nothing with his goods but sin. He is like the horse that chooses to drink dirty water rather than the water of the clear well. And as much as they give where they should not give, to them pertains the same curse that Christ should give on the day of doom to those that shall be damned.

The Vice of Gluttony

GLUTTONY
Sequitur de Gula

After Avarice comes Gluttony which is also expressly against the commandments of God. Gluttony is immoderate appetite to eat or drink or else to cater to the immoderate appetite and disorderly greed to eat and drink. This sin corrupts all the world as shown in the sin of Adam and Eve. Look at what Saint Paul says of Gluttony: "Many," he says, "go, of whom I have often said to you, and now I say it weeping, that are the enemies of the cross of Christ, for whom the end is death, and for whom their stomach is their god and their glory is in the confusion of those that devour earthly things." He that is accustomed to this sin of gluttony may not withstand any sins. He must be in the service of all vices for it is the devil's storehouse where he hides and rests. This sin has many forms.

DRUNKENNESS

The first is drunkenness that is the horrible burial place of man's reason; and, therefore, when a man is drunk, he has lost his reason, and this is a mortal sin. But truly, when a man is not inclined to strong drink, and perhaps does not know the strength of the drink, or has feebleness in his brain, or has travailled through which he drinks more, and is suddenly caught with drink, it is no mortal sin but venial. The second kind of gluttony is when the spirit of a man grows all troubled, for drunkenness relieves him of the discretion of his intelligence.

The third manner of gluttony is when a man devours his food and has no right manner of eating. The fourth is when, because of the great abundance of his food, the humors of his body are distempered. The fifth is forgetfulness through too much drinking, for

The Virtue of Moderation

sometimes a man forgets in the morning what he did in the evening, or the night before.

The distinctions of Gluttony are shown in other ways by Saint Gregory. The first is to eat before it is time to eat. The second is when a man gets too fussy over food or drink. The third is when he takes too much. The fourth is elaborate workmanship in the preparing and dressing of his food. The fifth is to eat too greedily. These are the five fingers of the devil's hand by which he draws men to sin.

MODERATION
Remedium contra pecccatum Gule
REMEDY AGAINST GLUTTONY

The remedy against Gluttony is abstinence, as Galen* says. But I do not hold it meritorious if he do it only for the health of his body. Saint Augustine wished that abstinence be done for virtue and with patience. "Abstinence," he says, "is worth little unless a man have good will thereto, and unless it be reinforced by patience and by charity and that men do it for God's sake, and in the hope of having the bliss of heaven."

The companions of abstinence are temperance that holds to the mean in all things; also shame that eschews all dishonesty, sufficiency that seeks no rich meat or drink, nor makes any effort toward the outrageous preparation of food; measure, also that restrains by reason the excessive appetite of eating; sobriety, that restrains the outrage of drinking; spareness that restrains the delicate ease of sitting long and comfortably at meals, and some folk stand of their own free wills to eat in less leisure.

LECHERY
Sequitur de Luxuria

After Gluttony comes Lechery for these two sins are so akin that often they will not be separated. God knows this sin is very displeasing to God; for he said himself, "Do no lechery." And, therefore, he put great pain against this sin in the old law. If a woman slave were taken in this sin, she would be beaten to death with sticks, and if she were a gentle woman, she would be stoned, and if she were a high priest's daughter, she would be burned, by God's commandment. Furthermore, for the sin of lechery, God drowned all the world at the flood. And after that he burned five cities with thunder and lightning and sank them into hell.

Now let us speak of this same stinking sin that men call adultery of wedded folk, that is to say, if one of them is married, or else both. Saint John says that adulterers should be in hell in a stinking burning of fire and brimstone; in fire for their lechery, in brimstone for the stink of their filth. Certainly the breaking of this sacrament is a horrible thing. It was made by God himself in Paradise, and confirmed by Jesus Christ himself, as Saint Matthew witnesses in the gospel, "A man shall leave father and mother and cleave to his wife, and they shall be two in one flesh." This sacrament symbolizes the knitting together of Christ and holy church. And God not only forbade adultery in deed but he also commanded that you should not covet your neighbor's wife. "In this command," says Saint Augustine, "all manner of covetousness related to lechery is forbidden."

Look what Saint Matthew says in the gospel, that "whosoever looks at a woman with lust has done lechery with her in his heart." Here you may see that not only is the deed forbidden but also the desire to

The Vice Of Lechery

do that sin. This cursed sin grieviously annoys him who is accustomed to it, first to the soul for it obliges it to sin and to the pain of unending death. And to the body it is also a grievious annoyance for it dries it and wastes it and defiles it and he makes sacrifice of his blood to the fiends of hell. It also wastes his possessions and his substance. Certainly it is a foul thing for a man to waste his possessions on women; yet it is a fouler thing than that when women, for such filth, throw away their property and their substance on men. This sin, says the prophet, despoils man and woman of their good reputation and all their honor; it is very pleasant to the devil for by that he wins most of this world. And just as a merchant is most delighted with the merchandise that gives him the most advantage, so the fiend delights in this filth.

This is that other hand of the devil with five fingers to catch people into his villainy. The first finger is the foolish gazing of the fool woman and the fool man, that slays, just as the basilisk slays folk by the poison of his gaze, for the covetousness of the eye follows the covetousness of the heart. The second finger is the villainous touching in a wicked manner. And, therefore. Solomon says, "whosoever touches and handles a woman will fare like him who handles the scorpion that stings and kills suddenly through his venom;" as he who touches warm pitch shall destroy his fingers. The third is the foul words that are like fire that before long burn the heart. The fourth finger is the kissing and, truly, he would be a great fool who would kiss the mouth of a burning oven or a furnace. And the more foolish are they that kiss wickedly, for that mouth is the mouth of hell; and these old dotard lechers yet will kiss, though they may not do, and defile themselves. Certainly they are like the hound who, when he comes to a rose bush or other bushes, though he may not piss, yet will heave up his leg, and make a pretence to piss. And many a man supposes that he may not sin in any lecherous thing he does with his wife; certainly that opinion is false. God knows, a man may slay himself with his own knife or make himself drunk with his own cask. Certainly, if it is wife or child or anything he loves more than God, it is his idol and he is an idolater. A man should love his wife with discretion, patiently and temperately, and then it is as though she were his sister. The fifth finger of the devil's hand is the filthy deed of lechery. Certainly, the five fingers of Gluttony the devil put in the stomach of a man, and with his five fingers of lechery, he grips him by the reins to throw him into the furnace of hell. There they shall have the fire and the worms that last forever, and the weeping and wailing, and the hunger and thirst, and the grimness of devils that shall torture them without respite and without end.

Of lechery, as I said, come diverse kinds, as fornication which is between man and woman who are not married; and this is a mortal sin and against nature. All that is hostile and destructive of nature is against nature. By my faith, the reason of a man also tells him clearly that it is a mortal sin, for God forbade lechery. And Saint Paul gives them the kingdom that is not due to any creature except to them that do mortal sin. Another sin of Lechery is to deprive a maiden of her virginity, for he that does that certainly removes a maiden from the highest degree there is in this present life and bereaves her of the precious fruit that the book calls the hundred fruit. I cannot say it any other way in English but in Latin it is *Centissimus fructus*. Certainly, he that does that is the cause of much damage and wickedness, more than any man can reckon; just as he some- times is the cause of all the damage that the animals do in the field that break the hedge or closure, through which he destroys what may not be restored. For certainly virginity may no more be restored than an arm that is cut from the body may return again to grow. She may have mercy, this I know well, if she does penance; but it shall never be that she was not corrupted.

And though I have spoken somewhat of adultery, it is good to show more perils that belong to adultery, to eschew that foul sin. Adultery is, in Latin, to sin in approaching another man's bed, through which those who were one flesh abandon their bodies to other persons. From this sin, as says the wise man, follow many evils. First is the breaking of faith, and faith is the key of Christendom. And when that faith is broken and lost, truly, Christendom stands vain and without fruit. This sin is also thievery for thievery is generally to take from a creature his things against his will. Certainly this is the foulest theft there may be, when a woman steals her body from her husband and gives it to an adulterer to defile her; and steals her soul from Christ and gives it to the devil. This is a fouler theft than to break into a church and steal the chalice, for these adulterers break the temple of God spiritually, and steal the vessel of grace that is the body and the soul, for which Christ shall destroy them, as Saint Paul says. Joseph greatly feared this theft when his master's wife asked him to do villainy, when he said, "Consider, my Lady, how my lord has placed under my ward all he has in this world, and none of his things are out of my power except only you who are his wife. And how should I do this wicked thing and sin so horribly against God and against my lord ? God forbid it!" Alas! All too seldom is such truth found nowadays. The third evil is the filth through which they break the commandment of Christ and befoul the author of matrimony who is Christ. For certainly, in as much as the sacrament of matrimony is so noble and so worthy, so much is it a greater sin to break it; for God made marriage in Paradise in the state of innocence to multiply mankind in the service of God. And, therefore, the breaking is the more grievious; often from the breaking come false heirs that wrongfully occupy people's heritages. And, therefore, Christ will put them out of the kingdom of heaven that is the heritage of good people. From this breaking often comes a time when people are wedded unaware or sin with their own kindred, and namely these same rascals that frequent the brothels of foolish women must be like a common privy where men purge their filth. What say you also of procurers that live by the horrible sin of whoredom and force women to give them a certain amount of the money from their whoredom, yes, sometimes using their own wife or child, these bawds ?

Certainly these were cursed sins. Understand also that Adultery is set rightly in the ten commandments between theft and manslaughter, for it is the greatest theft that may be for it is the theft of the body and the soul. And it is like murder for it cuts in two and breaks in two those that were made one flesh. And, therefore, by the old law of God, they should be slain. Nevertheless, by the law of Jesus Christ, that is the law of mercy, when he said to the woman that was found in adultery and should have been slain with stones, according to the will of the Jews, as was their law, "Go," said Jesus Christ, "and have no more will to sin," or, "sin no more."

LECHEROUS PRIESTS

Truly the vengeance of Adultery is rewarded by the pains of hell, unless it is dissolved by penitence. There are still more species of this cursed sin; as when one of them is religious, or both; or people who have entered orders such as subdeacon, deacon, or priest or hospitalers. And the higher he is in the order, the greater the sin. The things that greatly increase the sin are the breaking of their vows of chastity which they made when they were received into the order. And furthermore, it is true that holy orders is the chief treasure of God and his special sign and mark of chastity, to show that they have been enjoined to chastity which is the most precious life there is. These people in the orders are the special claim of God, the special retinue of God, and so when they commit deadly sin, they are the special traitors of God and the people, for they live for the people, to pray for the people and while they are such traitors, their prayer avails nothing for the people. Priests are angels by the dignity of their mystery; but, forsooth, Saint Paul says Satan transforms himself into an angel of light. Truly, the priest that is accustomed to commit mortal sin is an angel of darkness masquerading as an angel of light. He seems like an angel of light but really he is an angel of darkness. Such priests are the sons of hell, as shown in the Book of Kings that they were the sons of Belial, that is the devil. Belial is to say "without judge;" and so are they. They think that they are free and have no judge any more than a free bull that takes a cow that he likes in the town. So they fare with women. For just as a free bull is enough for all the town, so is a wicked priest enough corruption for a whole parish or for a whole country. These priests, as the book says, do not show the mystery of the priesthood to the people; they do not know God. They were not pleased, as says the book, with cooked meat that was offered to them but by force took the meat that was raw. These scoundrels are not pleased with the roasted meat and boiled meat that the people feed them with with great reverence but they must have the raw meat of folk's wives and daughters. And certainly the women who consent to their harlotry do great wrong to Christ, to holy church, and to all the saints, and to all souls, for they take away from them, those who should worship Christ and holy church, and pray for Christian souls. And, therefore, such priests and their lovers, also, who consent to such lechery have the curse of all the Christian court, until they amend their ways.

The third kind of Adultery is between a man and his wife when they take no consideration in their union except for their carnal pleasure, as says Saint Jerome, and they think of nothing except that they are united; because they are married, all is good enough, it seems to them. But over such people, the devil has power as the angel Raphael said to Tobias, for in their uniting, they put Jesus Christ out of their hearts, and give themselves to all filth.

The fourth species is the uniting of those who are related, or related by marriage, or else with those that their fathers or relatives have dealt with in the sin of lechery. This sin makes them like dogs who take no note of kindred. And certainly, relationships are of two kinds: spiritual and fleshly; spiritual are those dealing with godparents. For just as he that engenders a child is his his fleshly father, so is a godfather a spiritual father. A woman may not join with her godson any more than with her own fleshly brother.

SODOMY

The fifth species is an abominable sin of which no man should speak nor write; nevertheless, it is referred to openly in Holy Scripture. This cursedness men and women do with diverse intentions and in diverse manners. But though holy scripture speaks of this horrible sin, certainly holy scripture may not be defiled any more than the sun that shines on the dunghill.

Another sin pertaining to lechery comes in sleeping and this sin often comes to those who are virgins and also to those who are corrupt. This sin men call pollution; it comes in four ways. Sometimes in languishing of the body for the humors are too rank to inhabit the body of man; sometimes from infirmity because of the feeble power to retain virtue, as physic might cause; sometimes from too much food and drink; sometimes from wicked thoughts that are in a man's mind when he goes to sleep, which may not be without sin; so men must be wise, or else they may sin very seriously.

CHASTITY AND CONTINENCE
Remedium contra peccatum luxurie
REMEDIES AGAINST LECHERY

Now comes the remedy against lechery: that is chastity and continence that restrain all the lawless movements that come from carnal desires. And he shall have the greater merit who most restrains the wicked heat of the desire for this sin. And this is of two kinds; that is to say chastity in marriage and chastity in widowhood. Now you shall understand that matrimony is the lawful uniting of a man and a woman who, by virtue of the sacrament, receive the bond by which they may not be separated all their lives, that is to say, while they both live. This, as the book says, is a very great sacrament. God made it, as I have said, in paradise and willed himself to be born in marriage. And to sanctify marriage, he attended a wedding where he turned water into wine, which was the first miracle that he performed on earth before his disciples. The true effect of marriage cleanses from fornication and replenishes holy church with good lineage, for that is the end of marriage; and it changes mortal sin to venial sin between those who are wed and makes the hearts as well as the bodies one. This is the true marriage that was established by God before sin began, when the natural law was in the right position

The Virtue of Chastity

in paradise and it was ordained that one man should have but one woman, and one woman but one man, for many reasons, as says Saint Augustine.

First because marriage is the symbol of the union of Christ and holy church. And the other is that a man is the head of a woman; by all means, it should be so. For if a woman had more men than one, then she would have more heads than one, and that would be a horrible thing before God. And also, a woman might not please too many people at once. And also, there would never be peace nor rest among them; for each would seek his own thing. And furthermore, no man would know his own progeny and who should have his heritage; and the woman would become less beloved from the time she was joined to many men.

Now we come to how a man should treat his wife, namely in two things, with sufferance and with reverence, as shown by Christ when he first made woman. He did not make her from the head of Adam, for she should not claim great lordship. For when the woman has the mastery, she makes much confusion. There is no need to give examples of this; the day to day experience should suffice. And certainly, God did not make woman from the foot of Adam, for she should not be held too low; for she cannot suffer patiently. God made woman from the rib of Adam for woman should be a comrade to man. Man should treat his wife with faith, with truth, and with love; Saint Paul says a man should love his wife as Christ loved holy church, loved it so well that he died for it. So a man should for his wife if there were need.

Now a woman should be subject to her husband, as Saint Peter tells. First in obedience. And also, as the law says, as long as a woman is a wife, she has no authority to swear nor to bear witness without the permission of her husband who is her lord; moreover, he should be so with reasonableness. She should also serve him in all honesty and be modest in her dress. I know well that they should try to please their husbands but not by the fanciness of their dress. Saint Jerome says, "Wives that array themselves in silk and precious purple do not clothe themselves in Jesus Christ." Consider what Saint John says in this matter also. And Saint Gregory also says that "no creature seeks precious array but for vainglory, to be honored before the people." It is great folly for a woman to be very well dressed outwardly and within herself to be foul. A wife should also be moderate in her looks, her bearing, her language, and discreet in all her words and deeds. And above all worldly things, she should love her husband with all her heart and be true to him with her body. So should a husband also be to his wife. For since all the body is the husband's, so should the heart be or between the two there is no perfect marriage.

Then men should understand that a man and his wife cohabit for three reasons. The first is the intention of bearing children to the service of God. For surely that is the ultimate reason for matrimony. Another is to each give the other the delight of their bodies, for neither has the power over his own body. The third is to eschew lechery and villainy. The fourth is, forsooth, deadly sin. To the first, it is meritorious; the second is also, for, as says the law, she has the merit of chastity that gives her husband the debt of her body, even though it be against her liking and the desire of her heart. The third manner is venial sin, and, truly, there scarce may be any of this without venial sin because of the corruption and the pleasure. The fourth manner is to be understood as when they cohabit only for carnal love and not for any of the previous reasons, but to enjoy burning delight, they never reckon how often. Truly it is mortal sin, and yet, sadly, some people endeavor to do even more than is sufficient for their appetite.

The second manner of chastity is to be a clean widow and eschew the embraces of a man and desire the embrace of Jesus Christ. These are those that have been wives and have lost their husbands, and also women who have done lechery and been relieved by penitence. And certainly if a woman could keep herself always chaste by the license of her husband so that she never give even one occasion that he could be offended by, it would be a great merit to her. These kinds of women that observe chastity must be clean in heart as well as in body and in thought, and modest in clothing and in countenance; and be abstemious in eating and in drinking and in deed. They are the vessel or the box of the blessed Magdelene that fill holy church with a sweet fragrance.

The third kind of chastity is virginity, and it behooveth that she be holy of heart as well as clean of body. Then she is the spouse of Jesus Christ and she is like the life of angels. She is the pride of this world and equal to the martyrs; she has within her what tongue may not tell nor heart know. A Virgin bore Our Lord Jesus Christ and he was a virgin himself.

Another remedy against lechery is to withdraw from such things as give occasion to this villany as leisure, eating and drinking. For certainly, when the pot boils too high, the best remedy is to remove it from the fire. Sleeping long in great quiet is also a great source of nourishment to lechery.

Another remedy against lechery is for a man or a woman to eschew the company of those by whom they are tempted; for though they may resist the deed, yet there is great temptation. Truly, a white wall, though it not catch fire fully from a lighted candle, yet the wall is blackened by it. Often I read that no man should trust in his own perfection unless he is stronger than Samson, holier than David, and wiser than Solomon.

Now after I have explained to you, as well as I can, the seven deadly sins, and some of their branches and their remedies, truly, I would if I could, explain the ten commandments. But such a noble doctrine I leave to theologians. Nevertheless, I hope to God they are, each and all, touched upon in this treatise.

Sequitur secunda pars Penitence
Here follows the Second Part of Penitence

REQUIREMENTS FOR CONFESSION

Now, in as much as the second part of Penitence stands upon the Confession by mouth, as I began in the first chapter, I say, Saint Augustine says: "Sin is every word and every deed and all that men desire against the law of Jesus Christ; and this is to sin in heart, in mouth, in deed, by the five senses that are sight, hearing, smelling, tasting or savoring, and feeling." Now it is good to understand the circumstances that greatly aggravate every sin. You should consider who you are that do the sin, whether you are male or female, young or old, noble or serf, free or servant, well or sick, wedded or single, of an order or not, wise or foolish, cleric or secular; whether she is of your kindred, bodily or spiritual, or not; whether any of your relations have sinned with her, or not, and many more things.

Another circumstance is this: whether it be fornication or adultery or neither; incest or not, a virgin or not, homicide or not, horrible great sins or small, and how long you have continued in sin. The third circumstance is the place where you committed the sin; whether it was in another man's house or your own; in a field, in church or in a churchyard, in a dedicated church, or not. If the church be consecrated and a man waste his nature within that place by way of sin or wicked temptation, the church is interdicted until it is reconciled by the bishop. And the priest should be interdicted that did such a villainy; to the end of his life he should never sing mass and if he did, he would do mortal sin every time he sang the mass.

The fourth circumstance is that involving go-betweens or messengers, as for enticements, or for consent to bear company with fellowship; for many a wretch will go to the devil of hell for encouraging sin. Wherefore they that incite the sin or consent to the sin are partners to the sin and to the damnation of the sinner.

The fifth circumstance is how many times he has sinned, if it be in his mind, and how often he has fallen. For he that often falls into sin despises the mercy of God and increases his sin and is unkind to Christ and grows weaker in withstanding sin and sins the more easily, and is more reluctant to go to confession to him that is his confessor. For those folk who fall again into their old follies either leave their old confessors entirely or else make their confessions in diverse places, but truly, such deserve no mercy from God for their sins.

The sixth circumstance is when man sins by temptation, and whether this is from himself or from the inciting of other people or if he sin with a woman by force or by her own consent or if the woman, in spite of all she could do, was forced or not. This she should tell, for covetousness, for poverty, and if it was her procuring or not, and such kinds of provisions.

The seventh circumstance is in what manner he has done his sin or how she has allowed what people have done to her. And the man shall tell the same plainly with all the circumstances; and whether he has sinned with common brothel women or not; or done his sin during holy times or not, during times of fast or not, before his confession or after his last confession; and has perhaps, therefore, broken his penance; by whose help and whose counsel, by sorcery or craft; all must be told. All these things, whether they be great or small, weigh down the conscience of a man. And the priest that is your judge may better be advised about his judgement in giving penance, after your contrition. For understand well, after a time when man has defiled his baptism by sin, if he would come to salvation, there is no other way but by penitence and confession and satisfaction; and particularly by the two, if there is a priest to whom he may go to confession and third, if he have the life to perform it.

Then man should look and consider that if he would make a true and profitable confession, there must be four conditions. First there must be sorrowful bitterness of heart, as King Hezekiah said to God, "I will remember all the years of my life in the bitterness of my heart." This condition of bitterness has five signs. The first is that the one making confession must be ashamed to cover or hide his sin for he has offended his God and defiled his soul. And of this Saint Augustine says "the heart travailes for shame of his sin." If he has great shame, he is worthy to have the great mercy of God. Such was the confession of the publican who would not even lift his eyes to heaven for he had offended the God of heaven; for this shame he, at once, had the mercy of God. And, therefore, Saint Augustine says shamefaced people are next to forgiveness and remission.

Another sign is humility in confession of which Saint Peter says , "Humble yourself under the might of God." The hand of God is mighty in confession, for thereby God forgives you your sins, for he alone has the power. And this humility should be in the heart and in outward signs, for just as he has humility before God in his heart, just so he should humble his body outwardly to the priest that sits in God's place. Since Christ is the sovereign and the priest is the mediator between Christ and the sinner, and the sinner is the least, then the sinner should not sit as high as his confessor but kneel before him or at his feet, unless illness prevents him. For he should not take care who sits there, but in whose place he sits. A man who has tres- passed against a lord and comes to ask mercy and make peace and sets himself down next to the lord would be thought outrageous and not worthy to have remission or mercy so soon.

The third sign is how your confession should be full of tears, if a man may, and if a man may not weep with his bodily eyes, let him weep in his heart. Such was the confession of Saint Peter, for after he had forsaken Christ, he went out and wept full bitterly.

The fourth sign is that he not let shame prevent him from his confession. Such was the confession of Magdelene that did not hesitate, for shame of those who were at the feast, to go to our Lord Jesus Christ and make her sin known to him.

The fifth sign is that a man or woman be obedient in receiving the penance that is enjoined to him for his sins, for certainly, Jesus Christ, for the guilt of man, was obedient to the death.

The second condition of true confession is that it be quickly done. For certainly, if a man had a deadly wound, the longer he tarried to try to cure it himself, the more it would corrupt and hasten his death, and also the wound would be harder to heal. And so it is with sin that is hidden in man a long time. Certainly a man should quickly show his sins for many reasons; for fear of death that often comes very suddenly and there is no knowing the time it will be, nor in what place; and also the prolonging of sin draws in another sin; and also the longer he waits, the further he is from Christ. If he waits until his last day, he may scarcely confess, nor remember all his sins nor repent of them because of the seriousness of his deadly sickness. And as much as he has not listened to Jesus Christ in his life when he has spoken, on his last day he shall cry to him and scarcely will Christ listen to him.

Understand, this condition must have four things. The confession must be prepared for and deliberated, for wicked haste gives no profit; a man must have knowledge of his sins, be they pride or envy, and so forth with the kinds and circumstances, and he must have thought over in his mind the number and the greatness of his sins and how long he has lain in sin and also, he must be contrite and have a firm purpose, by the grace of God, never to fall into sin, and also that he fear and watch over himself that he flee the occasion of the sins to which he is inclined.

And also you shall confess all your sins to one man and not part to one man and part to another; that is to understand that to intend to divide your confession because of shame or pride is nothing but to strangle your soul. For Jesus Christ is entirely good; in him is no imperfection; and therefore either he forgives all perfectly or never a part. I am not saying that if you are assigned to the *penitauncer* (confessor who assigns penance) for a certain sin, that you are bound to show him all the rest of your sins of which you have been shriven by your curate, unless it pleases you in humility; this is not dividing your confession. Nor do I say, as I speak of division of confession, that if you have freedom to confess to a discreet and honest priest whom you like, and by permission of the curate, you may not well confess to him all your sins. But let no fault be hidden, no sin untold, as far as you can re-member. And when you go to confession to your curate, tell him all the sins you have commited since your last confession; that is not a wicked intention to divide your confession.

Also the very confession asks certain conditions. First that you confess of your own free will, not under constraint, nor for shame before people, nor for sickness, nor such things. For it is reasonable that since he trespasses by his free will, he confesses his trespasses by his free will; and that no other man tell his sins but he himself; he shall not refuse to admit or deny his sins; nor get angry with the priest for his admonishment to stop sinning. The second condition is that your confession be lawful, that is to say that you who confesses and the priest that hears your confession be truly in the faith of holy church; and that a man not despair of the mercy of Jesus Christ, as Cain or Judas.

And also a man must accuse himself of his own trespasses, and not another; he shall blame and reproach himself and his own malice in sinning, and not another. But nevertheless, if another man be the occasion or the tempter of his sin, or the state of a person be one in which his sin is aggravated, or else he may not confess plainly unless he tells the person with whom he has sinned, then he may tell it in such a way that his intention not be to denigrate the person but only to explain his confession.

You shall make no lies in your confession, out of humility, perhaps, saying you have done sins of which you were never guilty. For Saint Augustine says, "If you, because of of your humility, tell lies about yourself, though you were not in sin before, you are then in sin through lying." You must also show your sin by your own mouth, unless you be struck dumb, and not by letter, for you who have done the sin shall have the shame for it. You also shall not paint your confession with pretty, subtle words to hide your sin more, for then you beguile yourself, not the priest. You must tell it flatly, be it ever so foul or horrible. Also, you shall confess to a priest who is discreet in counseling you; you shall not confess for vanity, nor hypocrisy, nor for any cause except your duty to Jesus Christ and the health of your soul. You shall not run to the priest suddenly to tell him lightly, like one who tells a joke or a tale, but seriously and with great devotion.

And generally, go to confession often. If you fall often, you arise by confession. And if you confess oftener than once of sin of which you have been shriven, it is the more merit. And as Saint Augustine says, you shall have release and the grace of God more joyously, both from sin and from pain. And certainly, once a year at least it is lawful to receive the Eucharist, for certainly once a year all things renew.

Now I have told you of true confession, the second part of penitence.

Explicit secunda pars Penitencie, et sequitur tercia pars eiusdem. Here Ends the Second Part of Penitence and Follows the Third Part of It.

Canterbury Cathedral

SATISFACTION FOR SIN

The third part of Penitence is satisfaction and that is most generally by alms or bodily pain. Now there are three kinds of alms: Contrition of heart by which a man offers himself to God; another is to have pity on the defects of his neighbors; the third is the giving of good counsel and comfort, spiritual and bodily, where men have need, and especially in the providing of a man's food. And take note that man has need of these things, generally: he has need of food, he has need of clothing and lodging, he has need of charitable counsel and visiting in prison, and in sickness and in the internment of his dead body. And if you may not visit the needy in person, visit him by your message and by gifts. These are general alms or works of charity of those that have temporal wealth or discretion in counseling. You shall hear of these works on the day of doom.

You shall do these alms with your own proper things, quickly and privately if you can. But nevertheless, if you cannot do them privately, you shall not hesitate to do alms even though men see them, as long as they are not done for the thanks of the world but only for the thanks of Jesus Christ. For as Saint Matthew witnesses, " A city may not be hid that is set upon a mountain, nor do men light a lantern and set it under a bushel, but men put it on a candlestick to give light to the men in the house. just so shall your light shine before men that they may see your good works and glorify your father that is in heaven."

PRAYER

Now to speak of bodily pain; it is in prayers, in fasting, in watches, in virtuous teachings of prayer. You should understand that orisons or prayers are to be said with a pleading heart that addresses God and is expressed in outward word, to remove harm and to gain spiritual and lasting things, and sometimes temporal things; certainly in the prayer of the *Pater Noster,* Jesus covered most things. It is special for three things in his honor which make it more worthy than any other prayer; Jesus Christ himself made it; it is short so it can be said more quickly and held more easily in the heart and help one often; and a man would become less weary in saying it, and have less excuse not to learn it, it is so short and easy; and it covers, in itself, all good prayers. The exposition of this holy prayer that is so excellent and worthy, I leave to the masters of theology except this much I will say that when you pray that God forgive you your sins as you forgive those who trespass against you, be well aware that you are not without charity. This holy prayer releases venial sin and therefore it pertains especially to penitence.

The prayer must be sincerely said, and in true faith, and man should pray to God in an orderly, discreet, and devout way; and always a man should place his will subject to the will of God. This prayer must also be said with great humility, purely, and not to the annoyance of any man or woman. It must also be followed by works of charity. It avails against the vices of the soul for as Saint Jerome says, "By fasting we are saved from the vices of the flesh and by prayer from the vices of the soul."

FASTING

Next you should understand that bodily pain abides in watching, for Jesus Christ said, "Watch and pray that you enter not into wicked temptation." You should understand also that fasting abides in three things: in forbearing from bodily meat and drink, and in forbearing from worldly jollity, and in forbearing from mortal sin, that is to say that a man should keep from deadly sin with all his might.

And you should understand also that God ordained fasting and there are four things that pertain to fasting: generosity to poor people; spiritual gladness of heart, not to be angry nor annoyed, nor grouch because he fasts; and also a reasonable hour to eat; eat with moderation, that is to say, a man should not eat untimely, nor sit too long at table to eat when he is fasting.

DISCIPLINES

You should understand that bodily pain is in discipline or teaching, by word, or by writing, or by example; also in the wearing of hair shirts or coarse cloth, or by wearing hauberk (coat of mail) on the naked flesh for Christ's sake, and such kinds of penances. But beware that such penances of the flesh do not make your heart bitter or angry or annoyed with yourself; for better to cast away the hair shirt than to cast away the surety of Jesus Christ. And therefore, Saint Paul says, "Clothe yourself as they who have been chosen by God in a heart of mercy, meekness, patience, and such kinds of clothing:" in which Jesus Christ is more apparelled than in hair-shirts or hauberks or armor.

There is discipline also in beating the breast, in scourging with cords, in kneeling, in tribulations, in suffering wrongs that have been done to you patiently, also in suffering from illness, or the loss of worldly goods or of wife or of child, or of other friends.

Then you should understand which things disrupt penance. These are of four kinds: fear, shame, hope, and despair, that is desperation. To speak first of fear for which he imagines that he can suffer no penance; the remedy against this is to think how bodily penance is but short and light compared to the pain of hell that is so cruel and so long that it lasts without end.

Now against the shame that a man has to confess, and also these hypocrites that pretend to be so perfect that they have no need for confession, against that shame a man should reason that he that is not ashamed to do foul things certainly should not be ashamed to do a fair thing, and that is confession. A man should also think that God sees and knows all his thoughts and his works; nothing may be covered nor hidden from him. Men should also remember the shame that will come on the day of doom to those who are not penitent and confessed in this present life. For all the creatures in heaven, on earth, and in hell shall see openly all that they hide in this life.

Now to speak of the hope of those who are negligent and slow to get to confession. It is in two manners. One is that he hopes to live long and purchase riches for his pleasure, and then he will shrive him, and as he sees it, then is soon enough to come to confession. Another is the presumption he has on Christ's mercy. Against the first vice he should think that our life has no assurance and also that all the riches in the world are chance and pass like the shadow on the wall. Saint Gregory says that it belongs to the great justice of God that never shall the pain cease for them who never would withdraw from sin willingly, but continued on in sin; for the same perpetual will to do sin they shall have perpetual pain.

AGAINST DESPAIR

Despair is in two ways: the first despair is in the mercy of Christ; the second is that they think that they might not long persevere in goodness. The first despair comes from him who thinks he has sinned so greatly and so often and lain in sin so long that he shall not be saved. Certainly against that cursed despair, he should remember the passion of Jesus Christ is stronger to unbind than sin is to bind. Against the second despair he shall think that as often as he falls he may rise again by penitence. And though he has lain in sin ever so long, the mercy of Christ is always ready to receive him into mercy. Against the despair that he could not persevere long in goodness, he should realize that the weakness of the devil will do nothing unless men allow him, and also he will have the strength of the help of God and all holy church, and the protection of the angels, if he wishes.

ETERNAL JOY

Then men should understand what the fruit of penance is; according to the word of Jesus Christ it is the endless bliss of heaven. Their joy has no opposition in woe or grief; all the harm of this present life has passed; there is safety from the pains of hell; there is a blissful company that rejoices evermore, each in the others' joy. The body of man that was foul and dark is more clear than the sun; the body that was sick, frail, and feeble and mortal is immortal and so strong and so well that nothing may injure it; there is neither hunger nor thirst nor cold; every soul is replenished with the sight of the perfect knowledge of God. Men may purchase this blissful reign by spiritual poverty, the glory by lowliness, the plenitude of joy by hunger and thirst, and the resting by travail, and the life by death and the mortification of sin.

THE END OF THE PARSON'S TALE

RETRACTIONS

Here the maker of this book takes his leave.

Now I pray all who listen to this little treatise or read it, that if there is anything in it that pleases them, that for that they thank Our Lord Jesus Christ from whom comes all knowledge and all goodness. And if there is anything that displeases them, I pray also that they attribute it to my own ignorance and not to my will that would gladly have said better if I had the knowledge. For our book says, "All that is written is written for our teaching," and that is my intent.

Wherefore, I beseech you meekly, for the mercy of God, pray for me that God have mercy on me and forgive me my sins; namely my translations and editings of worldly vanities, the which I revoke in my retractions: as is the book of *Troilus;* also the book of *Fame;* the book of *the xix Ladies*; the book of *the Duchess;* the book of *Saint Valentine's day of the Parliament of Birds*; the *Tales of Canterbury* that encourage sin; the book of *the Lion;* and many another book if they were in my remembrance, and many a song and many a lecherous lay; that Christ in his great mercy forgive me the sin.

But of the translation of Boethius' *Consolations,* and other books of the legends of the saints, and homilies and moralities and devotions, I thank our Lord Jesus Christ and his blessed Mother and all the saints of heaven, beseeching them that henceforth to the end of my life, they send me the grace to be sorry for my sins and to work for the salvation of my soul, and grant me the grace of true penitence, confession, and satisfaction to do in this present life through the benign grace of him who is king of kings and priest over all priests, who bought us with the precious blood of his heart, so that I may be one of them, on the day of doom, that shall be saved. *Qui cum Patre et Spiritu Sancto vivit et regnat Deus per omnia secula, Amen*

Here is ended the book of *The Tales of Canterbury,* compiled by **Geoffrey Chaucer**, on whose soul Jesus Christ have mercy. Amen.

APPENDICES

NOTES

1. The line numbers here and following refer to Robinson's Middle English edition: *The Complete Works of Geoffrey Chaucer*. F. N. Robinson, The Riverside Press, Cambridge, MA , 1933. The modernization is mine.

2. Chaucer was born between 1340 and 1344. That date is uncertain. The date of death on his tomb in Westminster Abbey is October 25, 1400. He is buried in what was, in later years, called "The Poet's Corner." It is probable that *The Canterbury Tales* were written toward the end of his life --- after 1387. (See **Chronology.**)

3.   Saint Thomas à Becket was the friend of Henry II, appointed by him to be Archbishop of Canterbury in 1162. As archbishop, he reformed his life, became devout, gave his possessions to the poor and became an ideal prelate to whom the poor had access in their troubles. However, Henry no longer influenced him and they disagreed on control of the church in England. While Thomas was saying Vespers on December 29, 1170, he was stabbed in the back by four men who claimed to be under orders from the king. The people were furious and Henry who disclaimed any responsibility for Thomas's murder, nevertheless did public penance on the steps of the Canterbury cathedral. For the next 418 years, until the time of Henry VIII, his shrine was revered. Frequent Pilgrimages were made there. When Henry VIII destroyed the shrine in 1538, he apparently destroyed and scattered the remains of Saint Thomas and confiscated two truckloads of treasures the people had left at the cathedral as offerings. He also destroyed every kind of art work reminiscent of Catholicism.

4.   At least two modern translations could probably be found in university libraries: J. U. Nicolson, *Canterbury Tales,* Covici Friede, Inc., Garden City Publications, NY, 1934, and Frank

Ernest Hill, *The Canterbury Tales,* The Heritage Press, The George Macy Companies, Inc., Longman's Green and Company, 1946. (Omits the Prioress's Tale.)

5. Boethius was a Roman Philosopher who lived from 480 to 524. He was interested in the Greek philosophers from a Christian viewpoint. His *Consolations of Philosophy* which Chaucer translated was reflective more of Plato and Seneca than Aristotle. The *Consolations* had a great influence on Chaucer which can be seen in his works, as Robinson points out, p. 374.

6. St. Raymond of Penneforte was the third general of the Dominican order. He lived one hundred years and accomplished many good works including the founding, with St. Peter Nolasco in 1218, of the Order of Mercedarians for the redemption of captives from the Mohammedans. He wrote the *Summa de poenitentia*, a source of *The Parson's Tale*, in the 1220's. He died in 1275.

William Peraldous was a French Dominican, a Doctor of the University of Paris, who wrote an encyclopaedia of the vices, the *Summa vitiorum*, another source for *The Parson's Tale*, in 1236.

Chaucer also used the *Summa virtutum de remediis anime,* a work on the virtues as the remedies to correct sin. It was written around 1240 but the authorship is undetermined. (See **Bibliography.**)

7. John 3:5; Matthew 28; 19

8. Aristotle, Greek Philosopher (384-322 B.C.), pupil of Plato, noted for work on physics, ethics, politics, etc.; deductive logic based on the syllogism; more empirical in his thinking than Plato, his teacher. Plato saw reality as being in ideas and concepts; the objects of perception being the manifestations of concepts or ideas (see **Universals**).

9. Helen Cooper, *The Canterbury Tales*, Oxford University Press, NY 1991, p 397.

10. Three in honor of the Blessed Trinity.

11. The Middle English word *shrive, shriven,* encompassed contrition,confession and satisfaction. It is still found in literature and poetry (such as Coleridge's "The Rhyme of the Ancient Mariner")

12. In 1215 the Fourth Lateran Council established seventy disciplines, one of which was that confession should be made at least once a year. This decision fostered studies and treatises such as we mentioned as sources for *The Parson's Tale.*

13. There has been some discussion about the word "myrie", line 46 of the Parson's prologue, because "merry " does not seem to fit his tone. Robinson and others seem to think it was the Parson's attempt at "his little joke." It may be that he intended a Medieval connotation of the word --- such as "glad" or "pleasing" or "agreeable" in the sense that it was inclined toward hope of heaven.

14. The Fathers of the Church are those teachers who wrote in the early ages of Christianity. Some of the Fathers have been designated by the Church as Doctors because of the excellence of their lives and their theological writings. The most recent Doctor of the Church is Saint Alphonsus Maria de Ligouri who died in A. D. 1787.

15. John of Gaunt (1340-1399), the son of Edward III, was the Duke of Lancaster, the founder of the House of Lancaster, the father of Henry IV who ruled from 1399 to 1413.

16. The dates are speculation, starting with Skeat's selection of the year 1387; some modern scholars calculate a date from

the length of shadows cast during the ascent of Libra mentioned in the Parson's Prologue or from the Introduction to *The Man of Law's Tale*. The pilgrimage is fictitious and all Chaucer tells us is that it was a "sweet April."

17. Edward III ruled 1312-1377; Richard II 1377-1399; Henry IV 1399-1413.

18. A chronological outline of Chaucer's life is given at the end of the notes. There is more information about his life than about other literary figures of that period because of his activities in public service.

19. The Ellesmere Manuscript is a very beautiful, complete, vellum manuscript, copied about 1410 in London, ten years after Chaucer's death and almost fifty years before the first printed book in Europe. It was kept in the library collection of the family of the Earl of Ellesmere from before 1620 until 1917 when it was bought at auction by Henry E. Huntington. Today it is on display in the Huntington Library, San Marino, California.

CHRONOLOGY OF CHAUCER'S LIFE

1340? 1344	Born to John Chaucer, a London wine merchant and Agnes, his wife.
1357	His name appears in the household accounts of Countess Elizabeth, wife of the Duke of Clarence, son of Edward III.
1359	Ransomed from captivity in France by the same household.
1360	Bearer of messages for the Duke in Calais and King Edward III.
1360? 1366	Marriage to Lady-in-Waiting, Philippa Roet.
1367	Granted a yearly pension of 20 marks.
1370?	Probable date of *The Book of the Duchesse,* since Blanche, Duchess of Lancaster died in the fall of 1369.
1372	His wife receives grant for service from John of Gaunt.
1374	Both get further grants of 10 pounds a year. Chaucer receives a grant of a pitcher of wine daily from King Edward III. Chaucer becomes Controller of Customs and Subsidy of Wools, Skins and Leather for the Port of London.
1375	Given custody of lands and person of Edmund Staplegate of Kent.
1376	Granted fine paid by John Kent for crime of smuggling.
1378	Leaves for mission in France, appointing John Gower as his attorney in his absence.
1377? 1381	Probable time of translation of Boethius.
1381	Probable date of composition of the poem *Parliament of Foules* celebrating the marriage of King Richard II in 1381.
1380? 1385	Probable date of *Troilus and Criseyde.*
1382	Controller of Petty Customs, Port, London.
1385	Justice of the Peace for Kent.

1386	Knight of Shire for Kent. Ends Customs office.
1386? 1387	Probable date for *Legend of Good Women*. Lived in Greenwich.
1387	Probable date of wife's death.
1389	Appointed Clerk of the King's works at Westminster.
1390	Appointed Clerk of King's Works at Windsor. Supervises building of grandstands for tournament at Smithfield. Appointed joint Forester North Petherton Park. Robbed twice near the Foul Oak in Kent while on business.
1391	Probable date of the *Treatise on the Astrolabe*.
1387? 1400	Probable date of *The Canterbury Tales*.
1394	Granted 20 pounds a year for life.
1398	Sole Forester of North Petherton Park. Probable time of move to Westminster.
1399	Granted by newly crowned King Henry IV, an additional 26 pounds plus. Probably wrote *Compleynt to His Purse* which was addressed to Henry IV as "Conquerour " of England.
1400	October 25. date of death on tomb in Westminster Abbey.

As you can see, all dates dealing with his writing are speculation on the part of scholars and dates of writings not mentioned are even more uncertain.

GLOSSARY

alms, money, food, etc. given to poor people.

Apocalypse, Book of Revelation; the ultimate destruction of evil by good.

benefices, an endowed church office providing a living for a clergyman, rector, etc.; the income from that office.

Calais, town on the sea in Northern France, the last English holding at the end of the Hundred Years War.

castellated, built with turrets, etc., like a castle.

clerk (from *clericus*, priest), in Chaucer's day, a scholar and clergyman.

Communion of Saints, the shared relationship and unity of the followers of Christ on Earth, in Heaven, and in Purgatory.

Compline, Night Prayer of the Divine Office.

concupiscence, strong, abnormal desire, especially sexual.

continence, self restraint, especially in sexual activity.

contumely, insulting, scornful attitude and language.

divines, theologians, in Chaucer's day.

doom, Judgement Day; a sentence of condemnation.

eschew, shun, reject, or avoid something harmful.

estates, in the Middle Ages, the three social classes with political responsibility:

　the **Lords Spiritual**, the clergy;

　the **Lords Temporal**, the nobles;

　the **Commons**, the merchants, farmers and working class.

examination of conscience, the self evaluation of past thoughts, words, and deeds that were transgressions against God in order to repent, confess, and ask pardon.

Galen, Greek physician and writer, A.D. 130-200.

guild, in Middle Ages, a union of men in the same trade or craft to protect members and uphold standards.

heraldry, the art or science of coats of arms, genealogy, flags, etc.

hire, to give the use of something in return for payment, or to pay someone to take over one's duties.

incarnate, to be made flesh

Jacob, son of Isaac, founder of the 12 tribes of Israel, also called Israel.

Job, Old Testament hero who endured great suffering but did not lose faith in God.

Joseph, here Jacob's 11th son, sold into Egypt by his brothers whom he later saved from starvation. (Book of *Genesis*)

largesse, generosity associated with nobility of spirit.

Merry, in Middle English meant *agreeable, pleasing.* It was from Old English, *myrae*, meaning *seemingly brief* --- not *jolly* as we use it today.

Nebuchadnezzar, king of Babylon who conquered Jerusalem, exiled Jews, destroyed the Temple in 586 B.C.

necromancer, one who practices black magic, claims to fortell the future by conversing with the dead.

patrimony, property inherited from father; also property endowed to a church.

perdurable, everlasting.

pertinacity, persistent, stubborn.

Prophets: those who speak for God.

> **David,** second king of Israel and Judah, c. 1000 B.C., author of the Psalms.
>
> **Ezekiel,** sixth century B.C., Major Prophet.
>
> **Isaiah,** eighth century B.C., Major Prophet of Christ's birth.
>
> **Jeremiah,** seventh to sixth century B.C., Major Prophet.
>
> **Micah,** eighth century B. C.
>
> **Moses,** leader who led Israelites out of Egypt, received the Ten Commandments.
>
> **Zechariah,** sixth century B.C., urged rebuilding of the Temple.

quick, lively, alive, vigorous.

Raphael, Archangel, one of seven angels who stand before the throne of God.

respite, interval of relief from pain, work, etc.

Saints: holy persons recognized by the church as being with God after their deaths, and capable of interceding with God for men on earth.

Ambrose, A.D. 340-397 Bishop of Milan, Feast Day, December 7.

Anselm, A.D.1033-1109, Archbishop of Canterbury, d. April 21.

Augustine, A.D.354-430 , Bishop of Hippo, North Africa, most important theologian during the Middle Ages. d. August 28.

Basil the Great, A.D. 330-379, Greek, Bishop of Caesarea, Doctor of Church, d. June 14.

Bernard, of Clairveaux, A.D.1090-1153, French abbot, restorer of the Cistercians, d. Aug. 20.

Gregory the Great, A.D. 540-604, Pope, d. March 12.

Ignatius, A.D. 50-110, Bishop of Antioch, martyr, d. Feb. 1.

Isidore, A.D. 560-636, Bishop of Seville, Scholar, d. April 4.

Jerome, A.D. 340-420, monk, scholar, translated Scripture into the Latin Vulgate from Greek and Hebrew. d. September 30.

John, here, John the Evangelist, Apostle, author of Last Gospel, Revelations, and three Epistles. Died at Patmos in A.D. 100. d. December 27.
(There are over 235 Saint Johns.)

John Chrysostom, A.D. 344-407, Archbishop of Constantinople, Doctor of the Church, d. January 27.

Paul, Apostle of Jesus converted on road to Damascus; author of fourteen Epistles, martyred in A.D. 67 at Rome. d. June 29.

Peter, leader of the Apostles, first Pope, martyred in A.D. 67 at Rome. d. June 29.

Thomas à Becket of Canterbury, Archbishop, martyred in A. D. 1170. d. December 29.

scruplous, conscientious; in a religious sense, overly conscientious.

secular, treating worldly things as distinguished from church-related.

Seneca, Roman statesman, philosopher, dramatist 4 ? B.C.-A.D. 65.

sentence, here, a way of thinking, opinion, sentiment; maxim.

simony, buying or selling sacred or spiritual things such as sacraments or benefices.

sodomy, abnormal sexual intercourse such as homosexuality or bestiality.

Solomon, King of Israel, son and successor of David, known for wisdom.

stave, here, a walking stick.

sufferance, power to endure pain; toleration.

Susanna, Old Testament heroine saved by Daniel.

temporalities, secular properties of the church such as revenues.

thraldom, slavery.

tithes, a tenth part of land use or income used for the support of the church.

Tobias, Old Testament book and hero of that book.

Universals, *Philosophical term*. Plato's Ideal Forms which, according to St. Augustine and the Medieval philosophers, have a Real existence as the archetypes of all created beings in the mind of God.
Under the influence of Aristotle (as found in the writings of Averroes) St. Thomas Aquinas questioned this position. Later philosophers moved on to the Nominalist position, denying any reality to such forms.

usury, lending money at interest; today, excessive interest.

vainglory, excessive pride, vanity, boastfulness.

vicar, at that time, a clergyman acting as deputy for a bishop.

BIBLIOGRAPHY

Bradshaw, Henry, *The Skeleton of Chaucer's Canterbury Tales* (London and Cambridge, 1868).

Bennett, J. A. W., *Chaucer at Oxford and at Cambridge* (Toronto and Buffalo, NY, 1974).

Cantor, Norman F., *Inventing the Middle Ages,* (Wm. Morrow and Company, New York, NY 10019, 1991).

Cooper, Helen, *The Structure of the Canterbury Tales* (University of Georgia Athens, GA,, 1984). 256 p.

_____*The Canterbury Tales*, Oxford Guides to Chaucer (Oxford and New York, 1991).

Donaldson, E. T., *Speaking of Chaucer* (London, 1970).

Hoffman, Richard L., *Ovid and the Canterbury Tales* (University of Pennsylvania, Philadelphia PA, 1966).

Howard, Donald L., *The Idea of the Canterbury Tales* (Berkeley and Los Angeles, CA., 1976).

Huppe', Bernard F., *A Reading of the Canterbury Tales* (State University of New York, Albany, NY, 1967). 245 p.

Ker, W. P. (d. 1923), ed., *Essays of John Dryden*, "Preface to the Fables" (Oxford, 1900).

Lawrence, William Witherele (d. 1958), *Chaucer and the Canterbury Tales* (New York, NY 1950).

Lumiansky, Robert Mayer, *Of Sundry Folk* (Austin, TX, 1955).

Marwick, Arthur, *Illustrated Dictionary of British History* (Thames and Hudson, New York, 1984). 319 p.

Morgan, Kenneth O., *The Oxford Illustrated History of Britain* (Oxford University Press, Oxford and New York, 1984). 640 p.

Petersen, Kate O. (Radcliffe College), *The Sources of the Parson's Tale* (Boston, MA, 1901).

Robinson, F. N., *The Complete Works of Geoffrey Chaucer* (Riverside Press, Cambridge, MA, 02138, 1933).

Seamnan, L. C. B., *A New History of England 410-1975* (New Jersey, 1982).

Slaves of the Immaculate Heart of Mary, *The Communion of Saints* (Still River, MA, 01467, 1978).

Wenzel, Siegfried, ed., *Summa Virtutum de Remedies Anime* (University of Georgia, Athens, GA, 1984).

Woods, William, *England in the Age of Chaucer* (Stein and Day, New York, 1976). 230 p.